MODERN FIGHTING AIRCRAFT
F-15
EAGLE

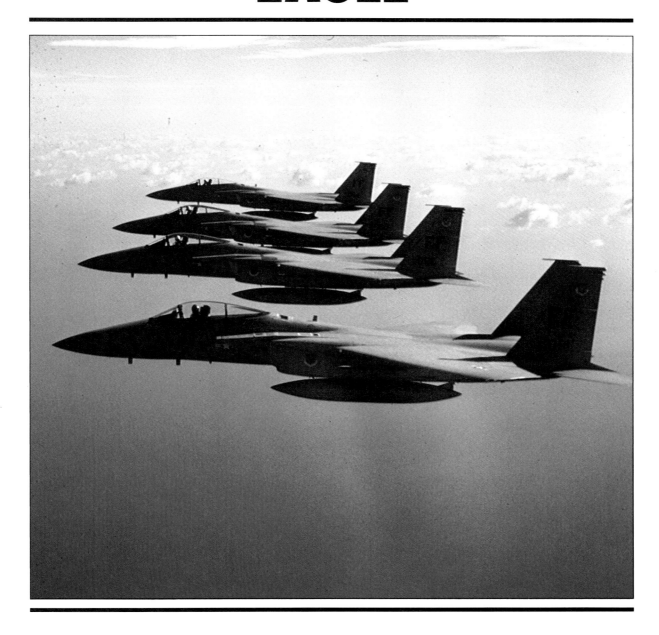

An Arco Aviation Book
Published by
PRENTICE HALL PRESS
New York

A Salamander Book

Published in 1986 by
Prentice Hall Press
A Division of Simon & Schuster, Inc.
Gulf + Western Building,
One Gulf + Western Plaza,
New York, NY 10023.

Previously published in U.S. by
Arco Publishing, Inc.

This book may not be sold outside
the United States of America and
Canada.

Library of Congress Cataloging-in-Publication Data

Gething, Michael J.
  F-15 Eagle
  (Modern Fighting Aircraft; 1)
  1. Eagle (Jet fighter plane). I. Title. II. Series.
UG1242.F5G47   1983   358.4'3   83-12240

ISBN 0-668 05902-8

Manufactured in Belgium.

First Prentice Hall Press Edition

10 9 8 7 6 5 4 3 2 1

All correspondence concerning the
content of this volume should be
addressed to Salamander Books Ltd.,
52 Bedford Row, London WC1R 4LR.

Contents

Acknowledgements

The author and editor are grateful to the
following individuals who have helped
in the preparation of this book: Geoffrey
Norris, Karen Stubberfield and Jeffrey
Fister of the McDonnell Douglas
Corporation; Major Dito Ladd, formerly
of the 36th TFW, USAF; and Colonel
Wendell H. Shawler, formerly Director
of the F-15 Joint Test Force.

The Powerplant chapter is based on
the equivalent chapter in the
companion volume *F-16 Fighting Falcon*
by Doug Richardson. The author is
further grateful to Don Parry, Lindsay
Peacock and Bernard Fitzsimons who
contributed the chapters on Avionics,
Deployment and Combat, and Structure
and Performance and Handling
respectively.

Author

Michael J. Gething is Managing Editor
of the Whitton Press *Defence* series of
publications and Editor of *Defence*.
Before joining the staff of the magazine
in 1976 he had worked for the Defence
Operational Analysis Establishment at
West Byfleet, and had been Assistant
Editor of the Royal Aeronautical Society
magazine, *Aerospace*.

Fascinated by aviation history since
his youth, he began his career as an
aviation journalist by writing on scale
modelling subjects. Although he has
less time to build models, he keeps in
touch with the scene through the
International Plastic Modellers Society.

In his spare time he is a squadron
officer with the Bracknell Squadron of
the Air Training Corps, having been
commissioned in the Royal Air Force
Volunteer Reserve (Training Branch) in
1972. Among his other books are *NATO
Air Power in the 1980s*, *Warsaw Pact Air
Power in the 1980s* and *Military
Helicopters*.

Credits

Project Manager: Ray Bonds

Editor: Bernard Fitzsimons

Designers: Tony Dominy
                Rod Teasdale

Diagrams: Arka Graphics
(© Salamander Books Ltd.)

**Three-view, cutaway drawing and
color profiles:** © Pilot Press Ltd.

Jacket: Brian Knight

Filmset by Tradespools Ltd.

Color reproduction by Bantam Litho Ltd.

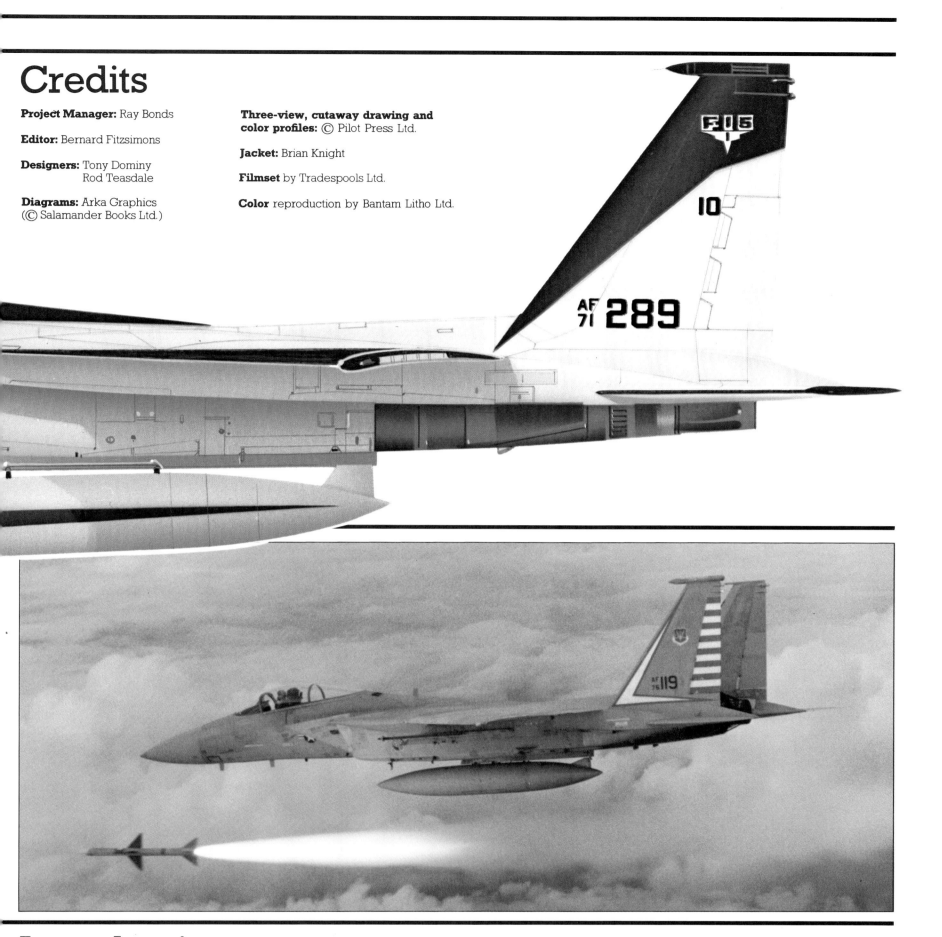

Introduction

Fighter aircraft have always held a special fascination, from the apparently flimsy scout biplanes of the First World War, through the legendary Spitfire, Mustang and Zero of the Second World War and the F-86 Sabre that fought over Korea to the F-4 Phantom of the 1960s. Even compared with such predecessors the F-15 Eagle sets a completely new standard, and one that only today is even beginning to be matched by the Soviet Union.

The Eagle's exceptional capabilities are the product of a combination of features. Two powerful F100 engines provide the 50,000lb (22,700kg) of thrust for record-breaking climb and acceleration; an airframe refined through thousands of hours of computer studies and wind-tunnel tests translates raw power into outstanding manoeuvrability; digital avionics and a powerful long-range radar enable targets to be detected at ranges of up to 100 miles (160km); and new versions of the medium-range radar-guided Sparrow and short-range heat-

seeking Sidewinder, along with a high-speed Gatling gun, form the Eagle's deadly claws. All these aspects are dealt with in authoritative detail in the following pages, along with accounts of the type's performance and handling qualities, its deployment and combat record with the Israel Defence Force Air Force and the future versions currently under development for the specialized ground-attack and anti-satellite roles.

The one major drawback with this exceptional aircraft is its price: only Israel, Japan and Saudi Arabia have so far found the wherewithal – and the official approval – to acquire their own F-15s, and not even the US Air Force can afford all the Eagles it would like. However, it was inevitable that the best fighter in the world, would also be one of the most expensive, and in terms both of current capability and of potential for development, it would seem that the size of the bill is equalled by the stature of the product.

Development

Confronted with a new generation of Soviet combat aircraft in 1967, while it was fighting in Vietnam with the 'second-hand' F-4 Phantom, the US Air Force began serious work on a new fighter of its own. Designated FX, and intended to provide air superiority in friendly and hostile airspace alike, the new design was to be optimized for combat, with the power and agility to overcome any current or projected Soviet opponent. In the resulting F-15 Eagle, with its unequalled combination of performance, firepower and sophisticated avionics, the USAF believes it has such a machine.

There are two adages which apply to the McDonnell Douglas F-15 Eagle: 'if it looks good, it is good' and 'if you design a good fighter, it can be adapted to other roles successfully'. The basic objective of the F-15 programme was, according to Major General Benjamin N. Bellis, F-15 System Program Director, "to efficiently acquire a fighter capable of gaining and maintaining air superiority through air-to-air combat". Although the Eagle has yet to be flown in action by the US Air Force it has fulfilled its purpose, again according to Maj Gen Bellis of being "a high performance, extremely agile aircraft to meet the projected threat of the late 1970s and early 1980s" at the hands of Israeli pilots over the Lebanon. The air-to-ground capability built into the original design is now being enhanced to produce the F-15E 'Strike Eagle', and the type is also being procured as an air defence interceptor to replace the F-106 Delta Dart.

The F-15 Eagle is the first air superiority fighter to stem from USAF requirements since the F-86 Sabre of 1948. The previous TAC (Tactical Air

Command) fighter was the F-4 Phantom II, designed for the US Navy and, together with the A-7D Corsair II, forced on the USAF by the circumstances of the Vietnam War. Having to procure Navy aircraft was anathema to the Air Force, and despite the success of both Phantom and Corsair, when the time came for a new tactical fighter the Air Force was determined that it should be of their own choosing.

New Soviet fighters
The genesis of the Eagle can, perhaps, be traced back to a Russian airfield at Domodedovo, near Moscow in July 1967. At an airshow there, in front of the world's press, the Soviet Union unveiled a new generation of combat aircraft. Of particular note were a swing-wing fighter, condenamed Flogger by NATO, and a high-speed, twin-fin fighter codenamed Foxbat, both from the famous Mikoyan-Gurevich (MiG) design bureau. Later information was to identify the Flogger as the MiG-23 and the Foxbat as the MiG-25, while a later ground-attack version of the MiG-23 was designated MiG-27 Flogger D.

The MiG-23 Flogger was a single-seat air-combat fighter powered by a single Tumansky R-29 afterburning tur-

bojet with a Mach 2.2 capability. Armed with a twin-barrel 23mm GSh-23 cannon and four air-to-air missiles – later known to comprise a pair each of AA-7 Apex and AA-8 Aphid AAMs – its range of 1,200 miles (1,930km) and service ceiling of 61,000ft (18,600m) made it a potent fighter. It was to supplement the MiG-21 Fishbed series of fighters, then in their second and now in the third stage of their development.

The MiG-25 Foxbat was also a single-seater, but powered by a pair of Tumansky R-31 afterburning turbojets. Initially a missiles-only interceptor, with a pair of AA-6 Acrid (one infra-red homing and one radar homing) plus a single AA-7 Apex and a single AA-8 Aphid, it carried a high-power radar codenamed Fire Fox. It has a Mach 2.8 capability, could fly 1,610 miles (2,580km) and had a service ceiling of 80,000ft (24,400m). Initially the design was thought to have been a counter to the American B-70 Valkyrie bomber cancelled in 1961, but the Foxbat was continued as an air superiority and reconnaissance fighter. The implication was obvious to the Pentagon: here was a fighter that could prove immune to the standard USAF fighter of the day, the F-4 Phantom.

Above: Air superiority blue and dayglo orange paint scheme on one of the pre-production F-15s during the flight test programme.

The FX study
Work on a new air superiority fighter had begun within the USAF as a general feeling of need for an aircraft in the best traditions of the P-51 Mustang and F-86 Sabre. This was in the early 1960s, and by April 1965 the USAF fighter lobby were looking at a Fighter Experimental (FX) type. In October 1965 the USAF asked for funding of full scale studies, and two months later issued a Request for Proposals (RFP) for a Tactical Support Aircraft. The Concept Formulation Study (CFS) which came out of the RFP went to Boeing, Lockheed and North American Rockwell in March 1966, the McDonnell Aircraft Company (MCAIR) being one of the losers at this stage. However, none of the submitted designs was considered further, mainly due to the aerodynamic configurations and by-pass ratio of the powerplants.

From mid-1966 to autumn 1967 activity on the FX was minimal, although the USAF maintained its own CFS team in being until autumn 1968. The impact of the Domodedovo revelations was felt,

Below: Silhouetted against the setting sun, a pair of F-15As in the skies they were designed to dominate.

and in August 1967 a second RFP for a CFS was issued. This time the words Tactical Support Aircraft were changed to one – Fighter – and this time MCAIR, along with General Dynamics (formerly Convair) were awarded the six-month study.

Among the objectives set by the USAF was a speed range of Mach 1.5 to 3.0. General Dynamics offered both a variable geometry and a fixed-wing FX: MCAIR recommended a fixed wing, twin engines and a single crewman. This second CFS was completed in May 1968, and in September of that year the FX Concept Development was authorized. In the same month the RFP for Contract Definition stage was offered to the aerospace industry, and MCAIR, along with Boeing, Fairchild Hiller, General Dynamics, Grumman, Lockheed, Ling Temco Vought and North American, bid for the contract. By De-

cember 1968 only MCAIR, Fairchild Hiller and North American were in the running.

By now the FX was designated F-15 and the three contenders were hard at work. A Development Concept Paper issued by the USAF defined the overall parameters of the design, and justified it against pressure from the US Navy to take a modified version of their VFAX/ F-14 on four counts: it would be a single-seat, fixed-wing, twin-engined fighter of approximately 40,000lb (18,000kg);

Top left: The 60,000lb (27,000kg) variable-geometry proposal produced by MCAIR in early 1968.

Above left: slightly later design study with fixed delta wing.

there would be no competitive fly-off, as this was not thought desirable; the VFAX was not considered a suitable replacement for the F-4E Phantom, nor could the F-4E be modified to meet the threat; and an air-to-ground capability

Top: Variable-camber leading edges were envisaged for this wing form developed in early 1969.

Above: Wooden mock-up of the F-15 used for NASA wind-tunnel tests.

would be included, but only as an offshoot of the primary air-to-air role.

Initiated under the Total Procurement Package, the programme thus left a large volume of work for the contractors bidding. No hardware competition

Right: The first F-15A prototype airborne for the first time from Edwards AFB on July 27, 1972.

Below: A month earlier, the same aircraft was photographed before the roll-out ceremony at St Louis.

Above: The third development F-15A, used to test the avionics, is seen here in the markings of the USAF Flight Dynamics Laboratory Advanced Environmental Control System.

F-15 Project demonstration milestones

Preliminary design review	Sep 70
Radar contractor selection	Sep 70
Critical design review	Apr 71
Avionics review	June 71
Major sub-assembly tests	Jun 72
Engine inlet compatibility	Mar 72
First flight	Jul 72
Bench avionics complete	Sep 72
First aircraft performance demonstration	Sep 72
First airborne avionics performance	Dec 72
Fatigue test to reach one lifetime	Jan 73
Static test 2 critical concluded	Jan 73
Armament ground test	Jun 73
1g flight envelope	Aug 73
Fatigue test to reach 3 lifetimes	Dec 73
USAF evaluation summary	Dec 73
Equipment qualified	Mar 74
Category II aircraft and equipment in place	Mar 74
Training equipment in place	Oct 74
Fatigue test to reach 4 lifetimes	Oct 74
External stores flutter and release	Aug 74
AGE equipment in place	Oct 74
Category I flight tests complete	Nov 74
First aircraft delivered to TAC	Nov 74

meant an enormous amount of paper studies and documentation, while the contract itself had to include tooling, development, testing and production. Later, in response to criticism from Congress and the public over cost over-runs on the C-5A Galaxy and F-111 programmes, the USAF worked in demonstration milestones which the contractor had to meet before receiving the next stage of funding. These are listed in the accompanying table.

The bids were made by June 1969, and from July to December the USAF's Aeronautical Systems Division made their evaluation. Selection of the McDonnell Douglas bid was announced on December 23, 1969. Major General Bellis announced in Washington the next day that in the technical, operational, management and logistic areas McDonnell Douglas had been placed first. In addition he went on to say that the MCAIR price had been lowest of the three. Selection of the winning contractor was the responsibility of Secretary of

the Air Force Robert G. Seamans Jr, after hearing presentations from the F-15 source selection evaluation board and the source selection advisory council, neither of which made specific recommendations. Secretary Seamans' choice was favourably received throughout the USAF.

The initial contract called for 20 development aircraft: a preliminary batch of 10 single-seat F-15A (71-0280–71-0289) and a pair of two-seat trainer TF-15A (71-0290 and 71-0291, later redesignated F-15B) Category I versions; and eight Category II full scale development (FSD) aircraft in single seat F-15A form (72-0113–72-0120). The FSD batch were closely matched to the production configuration.

The first F-15 was rolled out officially at MCAIR's plant at St Louis on June 26, 1972 with due ceremony. In July it was taken apart, loaded into a USAF C-5A Galaxy transport and airlifted to Edwards AFB, California. There it was reassembled, checked out and prepared

Above: The second development TF-15, later redesignated F-15B, was flown for the first time on October 18, 1973, and has subsequently been seen in a variety of configurations.

for its maiden flight. On a typical Californian clear day, with blazing sunshine, MCAIR's Chief Test Pilot Irving Burrows took the first Eagle (USAF serial 71-0280) into the air on July 27, 1972.

The Eagle's missions

In the terms of the FX Development Concept Paper (DCP), the F-15 is "optimized for counter-air missions" operating as part of TAC. These missions, which come under the general heading of air superiority, include escorting friendly strike forces over enemy airspace, making fighter sweeps ahead of such a strike force, combat air patrol between friendly strike aircraft and enemy bases, and tactical air defence of friendly territory.

According to the DCP, the most difficult of these roles is combat over enemy airspace, where "the counter-air fighter must protect the strike force from enemy fighters while under the disadvantage of being in the enemy's GCI network and exposed to potential attack from his fighters, SAMs and AAA". It is no surprise, therefore, to learn that the DCP calls for the F-15 to be "superior in air combat to any present or postulated Soviet fighters both in close-in, visual encounters and in stand-off or all-weather encounters".

According to the DCP assessment, neither an improved F-4E, with new wings and engines, or a version of the VFX (F-14 Tomcat) for which a contract was placed in February 1969, were considered able to meet the FX requirement. USAF politics aside, the configuration as a carrier aircraft for the basic role of fleet air defence and its consequent cost ruled out the VFX. However, an 'escape clause' was written into the DCP, which considered a

Left: An August 1975 view of the second F-15B, seen here carrying out trials with the Fuel and Sensor Tactical (FAST) pack conformal fuel tanks on the intake sides.

F-15 pre-production aircraft flight test roles					
Serial	**First flight**	**Function**	**Serial**	**First flight**	**Function**
71-0280	Jul 27, 1972	Open flight envelope; explore handling qualities; external stores carriage	71-0285	May 23, 1973	Avionics tests; flight control evaluation; missile fire control
71-0281	Sep 26, 1972	F100 engine tests	71-0286	Jun 14, 1973	Armament and fuel stores tests
71-0282	Nov 4, 1972	Avionics development; calibrated air speed tests	71-0287	Aug 25, 1973	Spin recovery, high AOA and fuel system tests
71-0283	Jan 13, 1973	Structural test airframe	71-0288	Oct 20, 1973	Integrated aircraft/engine performance tests
71-0284	Mar 7, 1973	Internal gun, external fuel jettison and armament tests	71-0289	Jan 16, 1974	Tactical EW system, radar and avionics evaluation

Below: F-15B 71-0291 in the Bicentennial paint scheme worn by this much repainted Eagle during 1976 as part of the celebrations of 200 years of American independence.

further examination when "revised, detailed information on the tradeoffs between VFX-2 (with new engines and lighter avionics) and FX will be available to enable a decision as to whether to pursue one or both of these aircraft".

It is further interesting to note that the Eagle itself was later considered for adoption by the US Navy. This occurred in July 1971, when the Secretary of Defense asked the Navy to investigate the possibility of an F-15N, via the Systems Program Office. A minimum modification study by MCAIR to equip the Eagle for carrier operations increased the weight of the aircraft by some 2,300lb (1,043kg). The Navy Fighter Study Group III then did their own appreciation, disregarding the MCAIR data, which resulted in further weight increases and the addition of AIM-54 Phoenix AAM. In this configuration the weight and drag sent the performance down and the costs up to a level where the F-15N was deemed unacceptable.

The navalized Eagle made one more appearance before being finally re-

jected. Investigative testimony before the Senate Armed Services Committee's ad hoc Tactical Air Power subcommittee started new discussions on a modified Eagle for the Navy. This was in March 1973, at a time when the F-14 Tomcat programme was under pressure. Deputy Secretary of Defense Packard wanted to look at a lower-cost F-14, the F-15N and improved F-4s as alternatives for the Navy mission. The result was the formation of Navy Fighter Study IV, where these alternatives were discussed, and out of it came the concept of the Naval Air Combat Fighter to partner the F-14 in a maritime equivalent of the Air Force F-15/F-16 hi-lo mix. Ironically, MCAIR was selected as prime contractor on this programme, which involved navalizing the Northrop YF-17 as the F-18 Hornet.

Each of the ten pre-production Eagles was allocated a specific task in the flight test programme. Their roles were as outlined in the table. The first two-seater, 71-0290, was first flown on July 7, 1973, and was used for the two-seater evaluation. The second two-seater was flown on October 18, 1973. The first two-seater was slotted between the seventh and eighth aircraft, and since then every seventh aircraft built has been in two-seat configuration.

Right: The Bicentennial Eagle in flight, sporting the flags of the many countries where it had been demonstrated below the canopy.

Below: Back to a more familiar colour scheme, but still sporting an array of flags below the canopy, 71-0291 touches down with speed brake deployed.

Right: 72-0118, the sixth of eight full-scale development aircraft produced for the USAF's own Category II flight test and evaluation programme.

The first 12 Eagles were allocated to Category I of the test programme (now known as Contractor Development, Test and Evaluation) under the manufacturer's test pilots. The eight FSD aircraft allocated to Category II testing (now the Air Force Development, Test and Evaluation) were flown by a USAF Joint Test Force of Air Systems Command test pilots and Tactical Air Command fighter pilots. Category III of the test programme (now the Follow-on Operational Test and Evaluation) was conducted by the USAF. Later some of the Category I aircraft were passed on to the USAF.

By October 29, 1973, when the 1,000th test flight was flown by an F-15, 11 of the 12 Category I airframes were flying. Those aircraft had expanded the flight envelope of the Eagle to a speed of Mach 2.3 and a height of 60,000ft (18,300m). While development proceeded reasonably smoothly, it was not without its problems, and MCAIR Chief Test Pilot Irving Burrows and Colonel Wendell Shawler, the USAF's Director of the Joint Test Force 'went public' on a number of these in a joint lecture to the Society of Experimental Test Pilots in 1973.

The first problem discussed related to the stick force per g value. As a result of simulator experience prior to the first flight, it was thought that the aircraft might not be as nimble as expected, simply because of the stick forces. As designed, it was thought that these stick forces would be comfortable for manoeuvring, while not being so low as to suggest the chance of a pilot-induced oscillation or aggravate high g sensitivity. There are two sets of controls: a conventional hydromechanical system, and a Control Augmentation System (CAS). Both are capable of flying the aircraft, though the former was considered a back-up system in the event of the CAS failing.

The hydromechanical system determines the basic control deflections,

Below: An early production F-15A in the markings of the 58th Tactical Fighter Training Wing, based at Luke AFB, Arizona, and wearing the standard Compass Gray two-tone paint scheme.

Above: Underside view of the 43rd production F-15A, the 61st of all single-seat Eagles.

Below: One of two F-15Bs which, along a pair of F-15As, all from the 58th TFTW, were painted in a special attitude-deception three-tone grey camouflage scheme devised by aviation artist Keith Ferris.

Right: F-15Cs on the McDonnell Douglas production line in June 1981, when over 600 Eagles had been delivered to the USAF.

while the CAS operates over the hydro-mechanical system and modifies the control surface deflections which provided aircraft response in line with the stick position. In the mechanical longitudinal system a spring cartridge provided the linear force gradient. There was much debate as to what was the optimum setting for the cartridge, but as the evidence was based on simulator experience only there was some reluctance to make changes. Besides, it was thought unwise to lighten the stick forces too much in case the aircraft was accidentally overstressed. Thus with a stick force (ie the pressure required to be applied to the control column in order to move the control surfaces) of 3.75lb (1.7kg) per g, manoeuvres in excess of 6.5g required some 25lb (11.3kg) of stick force to initiate a response to control demand. In such high-g situations this meant some considerable strain on the pilot.

Modified stick forces

Early flight testing confirmed the initial simulation findings. With the CAS off the manoeuvring forces were too heavy for a fighter with the inherent capability of the F-15. With the CAS on these forces were more comfortable, but there was room for improvement. A dual-gradient longitudinal spring cartridge was evaluated, and found to be an improvement, while modifications were also made to the CAS pitch computer, enabling a satisfactory match between the CAS and the hydromechanical system. Flight testing of these fixes confirmed their suitability, and were incorporated in production aircraft. Forces around the neutral position are considered 'comfortable' at all speeds within the flight envelope, and there was no excessive longitudinal sensitivity or trend towards oscillation with the CAS either on or off. Pilots can now fly 6g manoeuvres one-handed with no trouble.

The lateral sensitivity of the Eagle also came in for some criticism. Although, again, it was recognized on the simulator, it was partially masked by the lack of physiological cues. The original specifications called for rolling capabilities in excess of previous accelerations. These could only be achieved by using a large amount of lateral control – quickly. This meant that lateral control surface deflections were 'sudden and big'. While the ailerons, with plus or minus 20deg of travel, are mechanically served, the differential stabilator (all-moving tailplane) is connected to both the mechanical and CAS circuits.

Normal smooth manoeuvring was highly responsive, but comfortable. However, any sudden small lateral movements of the stick, such as might be expected during formation flying, gun-tracking or air-to-air refuelling, caused an undesirable jerkiness resulting in a possible pilot-induced oscillation. While not as simple to correct as was the longtitudinal system, a two-point solution was arrived at. A dual-gradient force system coupled with a higher setting on the CAS transducer prevented the CAS from augmenting roll commands at small stick deflections was the first fix; the second involved a modification to the CAS in order to

Right: Tanker's eye view of a two-seat Eagle, with the refuelling boom positioned in the F-15's receptacle. In-flight refuelling has enabled Eagles to fly non-stop the 7,000 miles (9,620km) between Okinawa and Florida.

Above: Three brand new F-15As in flight early in 1976 before delivery to the 1st TFW at Langley AFB.

Below right: Streak Eagle easily beat the F-4's climb records, and was faster than an Apollo moonshot to 15,000m.

Streak Eagle world time-to-height records

Altitude	Time	Date	Previous time	Margin
3,000m (9,843ft)	27.57sec	Jan 16, 75	34.52sec (F-4B)	20 per cent
6,000m (19,685ft)	39.33sec	Jan 16, 75	48.79sec (F-4B)	19 per cent
9,000m (29,528ft)	48.86sec	Jan 16, 75	61.68sec (F-4B)	21 per cent
12,000m (39,370ft)	59.38sec	Jan 16, 75	77.14sec (F-4B)	23 per cent
15,000m (49,212ft)	77.02sec	Jan 16, 75	114.50sec (F4-B)	33 per cent
20,000m (65,617ft)	122.94sec	Jan 19, 75	169.80sec (MiG-25)	28 per cent
25,000m (82,021ft)	161.02sec	Jan 26, 75	192.60sec (MiG-25)	16 per cent
30,000m (98,425ft)	207.80sec	Feb 1, 75	243.86sec (MiG-25)	15 per cent

negate some of the roll rate demanded by small sharp deflection of the stick.

The need to retract the undercarriage into the fuselage led to a rather narrow track of 9ft 0¼in (2.75m) and a wheelbase of 17ft 9½in (5.42m). To have considered another configuration would have incurred an unacceptable weight penalty. The narrow track promised to produce a few problems, and these duly appeared during the flight testing. During crosswind landings the upwind wing would come up, causing the aircraft to tend to weathervane into the wind, and again drift downwind. Holding the nose up on landing only accentuated the problems, and so pilots always tried to get the nosewheel on the ground as quickly as possible.

The causes of the problems were soon identified. The first involved the aileron-rudder interconnect (ARI) system: as the stick was moved laterally (assuming a neutral or aft longitudinal position) rudder movement was initiated in sympathy. So, if the right wing came up and the stick was moved to the right to counteract it, the rudder motion would make the aircraft yaw to the right, and thus aggravate the tendency to weathervane. The second problem occurred with the stick aft, as if to hold the

nose up, when the aircraft systems washed out some lateral control. This had been designed into the controls so as to minimize lateral deflections of the stick at high angles of attack. As the pilots said, "Rolling out on the runway was not the place to reduce lateral control, particularly in a very lightly wing-loaded fighter with a narrow gear".

In these circumstances, the wind would blow the wing up, and the aircraft would start weathervaning. The normal response by the pilot would be to move the stick into wind, but this did nothing to level the wings, and succeeded only in worsening the yaw into wind, giving the pilot the impression that the aircraft wanted to tip up and over onto the downwind forward quarter. Once the nosewheel was down, the situation improved slightly, but all the characteristics remained to a lesser degree, and the resultant roll-out was described as 'uncomfortable'. The whole problem was exacerbated by the oleo struts on the mainwheels tending to stroke at different times in the roll-out and on a calm day, there could be a 2 or 3deg difference until the up-wing oleo would stroke. A further weak point was the low-gain steering on the nosewheel.

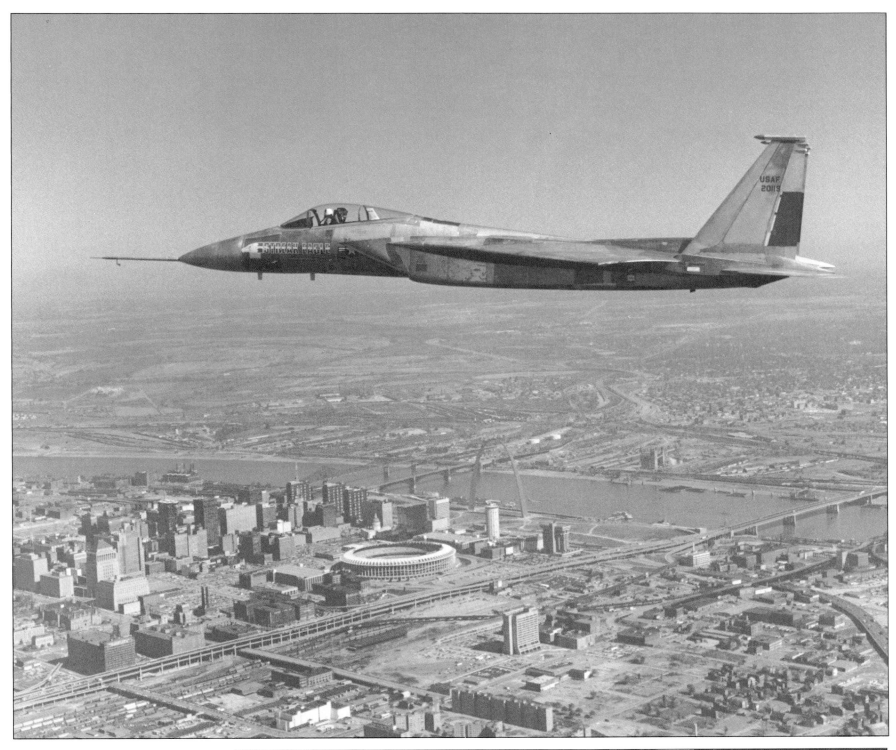

Above: The record-breaking Streak Eagle, 72-0119, over the familiar St Louis skyline.

The full plus or minus 15deg steering should have assisted three-point directional control, but because of the pedal-to-wheel deflection, long, strong legs were required to get positive response.

Considerable effort went into fixing the whole dilemma of cross-wind landing, and the Eagle can now accept such landings in 25–30kt crosswinds. To begin with, the ARI was all but eliminated on touch-down, as it had no essential function on the ground. The mechanical ARI was made to deactivate on sensing wheel-spin on the ground, which was almost instantaneous after touch-down. This effectively eliminated the effects of the ARI, but did retain it in a static condition until the ground checks were made. The CAS ARI was also largely eliminated during the roll-out in a similar fashion.

The mechanical lateral control wash-out with the stick aft was eliminated with the undercarriage down, while the gain was increased on the nosewheel steering so that the response was swifter.

Right: Major D.W. Peterson, who piloted the Streak Eagle to the 15,000m and 25,000m records on January 16 and 26, 1975, by the nose of the specially prepared F-15A.

Above: An early production F-15C refuels from a KC-135A tanker with an example of MCAIR's previous USAF fighter, the F-4, in attendance.

This fix was primarily to improve the taxying qualities of the Eagle, but the benefits to directional control on the runway were welcomed. The main-wheel oleo struts were significantly modified, so as to achieve a greater load stroke quicker on touchdown, while the remainder was taken up at lower speeds. Overall the Eagle had a

Below: One of the virtues of the F-15 is the minimal amount of ground support equipment needed, as illustrated in this view of pre-flight checks at a snow-covered base.

more solid feel following touch-down.

The time and effort expended on this series of fixes have paid dividends for Eagle operations. The 25–30kt cross-wind component allows crab angles of up to 12deg to be used on landing. With the nose held at 12deg pitch, for maximum braking effect, the Eagle's velocity vector is simply held straight down the runway with the rudder until the nose is lowered at about 80kt, where the nose-wheel steering takes over. All the pilot needs do is to fly down the runway using normal aerodynamic control until the nosewheel is lowered to contact with the ground.

The handling qualities of the F-15 Eagle in flight are described as 'excellent' using either the conventional hydro-mechanical system or the CAS to fly the

aircraft. However, several modifications known as Engineering Change Proposals (ECPs) were made, though by autumn 1974 only 36 had been recommended, of which 13 did not involve the Eagle itself. Of the 23 ECPs made to the aircraft, only three are externally visible: the raked wing tips, the dog-tooth stabilator, and the enlarged speed brake.

Early in the test programme MCAIR discovered a buffet and wing-loading problem at certain altitudes. After attempting to solve the problem with wing fences, the solution adopted was to remove 4sq ft (0.37sq m) diagonally from the wing tip to create a raked appearance. The cutting of the dog-tooth into the leading edge of the stabilator was the solution to a flutter

problem discovered in wind tunnel testing. This produced a minor shift in the coefficient of pressure and a change in the moment of inertia sufficient to remove the flutter. The enlargement of the speedbrake from 20 to 31.5sq ft (1.86 to 2.93sq m) allowed the required drag to be produced from lower extension angles, and removed a buffet caused by the original brake at the desired drag configurations (and higher extension angles).

Radio-controlled models

One of the more interesting aspects of the F-15's flight test programme was the use of large glider models of the Eagle, which were dropped from a Boeing B-52 of the NASA Flight Research Center flying at 45,000ft (13,700m) at 175kt. Termed 'remotely piloted research vehicles', these models were built of aluminium and glass fibre to three-eights scale, having a wing span of 16ft 1¼in (4.91m) and a length of 23ft 10¾in (7.28m) and weighing some 2,000lb (907kg). Radio-controlled from the ground, they performed their manoeuvres, deployed a parachute and were recovered in mid-air by a helicopter. Among their tasks were to conduct high angles of attack, stalling and spinning manoeuvres ahead of the live flight tests performed by the eighth development Eagle.

All these ECPs, many of a minor nature, have contributed to making a good flying aircraft into a fighter with excellent handling qualities. Following its first flight, the F-15 Eagle met all its milestones on time with one exception: because of technical problems concerned with F100 engine durability tests, this part was some months late. The test programme's deliberately slow pace was, according to Major General Bellis, able to provide "a significant capability to profit from information derived from the initial and intensive ground-test programme and the current joint Air Force and contractor F-15 flight test activities". Such a pace is totally in keeping with the 'test before fly' and 'fly before buy' attitude adopted by the USAF in their procurement procedure.

Final proof of the new fighter's capabilities was provided by Operational Streak Eagle, a joint USAF/MCAIR operation to break a number of time-to-height world records, previously held

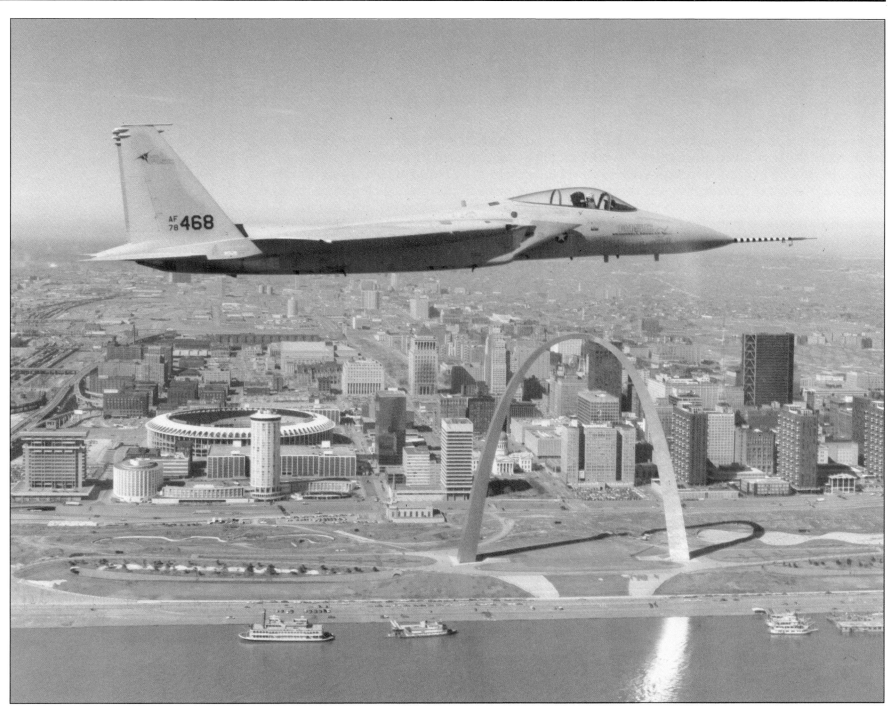

Above: St Louis again forms the background for this February 1979 view of the first F-15C before its delivery to TAC.

by the F-4 Phantom and Soviet MiG-25 Foxbat. The 19th pre-production aircraft (the 17th single-seater) was totally stripped down: radar, cannon, missiles, tail hook, utility hydraulic system, one of the generators, and several actuators were

Below: Three-view drawing of the production F-15C; the upper side profile shows the two-seat F-15D. Without the FAST packs, the F-15C is externally identical to the A.

removed, along with the paint finish, leaving a bare metal aircraft. Between January 16 and February 1, 1975, Majors W. R. Macfarlane, D. W. Peterson and R. Smith established a total of eight new time-to-climb records flying from Grand Forks AFB. The Eagle was some 2,800lb (1,270kg) lighter than a standard production aircraft and only sufficient fuel was carried for the specific flight and return to the airfield.

The Category I and II flight test programme was completed by the delivery of the first production Eagle, a TF-15A (F-15B) to the USAF's Tactical Air Command at Luke AFB on November 14, 1974. On July 1, 1975, the first oper-

ational F-15 Eagle squadron within Tactical Air Command – the 1st Tactical Fighter Wing (TFW) – was formed at Langley AFB, and six months later, on January 9, 1976, this wing received its first aircraft.

As with most aircraft in production, improvements and refinements are constantly emerging. The current production models of the Eagle are the F-15C and F-15D, which replaced the single-seat F-15A and twin-seat F-15B respectively from mid-1979, when a total of 443 had been produced.

Externally there is no major difference between the two sets of Eagles. Internally, the APG-63 radar has been

improved by the addition of a programmable signal processor (PSP), details of which are given in Chapter 4; the fuel capacity has been increased by some 312.5USgal (260Imp gal/1,188 litre); and the aircraft has been modified to accept two conformal Fuel and Sensor Tactical (FAST) packs on either side of the fuselage, enabling thé internal fuel capacity to be increased by a further 1,523US gal (1,268Imp gal/5,788 litre) altogether.

The first F-15C Eagle flew on February 27, 1979, with the first F-15D following on June 19, 1979. These versions entered service with the USAF in September 1979, when the 18th TFW at Kadena AB, Okinawa, Japan, received their first squadron. The F-15C/D model represents the baseline from which the F-15 Multi-stage Improvement Programme (MSIP) begins. In addition to the enhancements already noted, the MSIP will take in a new programmable weapon control set, with provision for the AIM-120 AMRAAM, AIM-7M Sparrow and AIM-9M Sidewinder missiles; expanded electronic warfare (EW) equipment, including an enhanced radar warning receiver (RWR), an internal ECM system and the addition of chaff/flare launchers; and expanded communications facilities, Seek Talk, HF radio and provision for JTIDS. Although further versions with enhanced roles are under development, the F-15C/D model of the Eagle remains the current production standard, and is likely to continue as such in the near term.

Structure

Thousands of hours of computer studies and wind-tunnel tests went into the F-15's design; billions of dollars have been spent on building the aircraft and its essential systems. Much of this effort and expense was devoted to keeping the basic structure as simple as possible, for maximum survivability in combat and ease of maintenance on the ground. In service, the Eagle may not have quite matched its designers' expectations, but an outstanding safety record and an improving rate of availability demonstrated by Tactical Air Command Squadrons are testimony to its basic soundness.

By mid-1967 the early conception of the FX as a 60,000lb (27,000kg) variable-sweep multirole aircraft had been rejected in favour of a 40,000lb (18,000kg) fixed-wing fighter, and by September 1968, when the Contract Definition RFP was issued, a number of design criteria had been established. Several of these were directly concerned with structural features, while others involving specific operational requirements imposed their own indirect constraints on the physical details of the resulting aircraft.

Since the Eagle was to be used for air combat, a combination of high thrust-to-weight ratio and low wing loading were stipulated, within the overall gross weight limit of 40,000lb. A high degree of survivability was called for in structure and subsystems, involving com-

prehensive testing of components used, along with extended component life and reduced maintenance requirements. And the single crew member, who would be provided with a comprehensive suite of automated avionics to enable him to carry out his mission unaided, was to be given all-round visibility.

Computer evaluations

During the preliminary FX design studies – which ultimately involved some 2,500,000 man-hours and resulted in 37,500 pages of documentation – MCAIR engineers carried out extensive computer evaluations comparing the weights of hypothetical aircraft of given cost resulting from a variety of basic design features. For example, if a two-

man, all weather avionic suite were installed, the gross weight of the aircraft was calculated as 46,000lb (20,865kg), while single-seat, clear-air avionics required a gross weight of only 31,500lb (14,290kg). Similar comparisons were made between theoretical aircraft with varying degrees of energy manoeuvrability and maximum speeds ranging from Mach 0.8 sea-level dash to a sustained Mach 2.7.

The parameters for the structural component of the computer evaluation were represented by an upper limit of 8g with 100 per cent fuel and a lower capacity for 6.5g with only 60 per cent fuel, giving respective gross weight figures of 41,500lb (18,825kg) and 38,000lb (17,235kg). The actual design limitation of 7.33g was achieved within

Above: Viewed from above, the contours of the Eagle fuselage clearly show the central pod and twin boom structural configuration.

the specified 40,000lb weight limit.

Considering that the external dimensions of the F-15 are marginally greater than those of the F-4 Phantom, it is remarkable that the maximum takeoff weight of the newer fighter should be nearly 6,000lb (2,700kg) less than that of its predecessor. Part of this reduction is a result of the lighter internal fuel load, which with the Eagle's more efficient

Below: June 1981, and among the F-15Cs and Ds on the MCAIR assembly line is the distinctive tail of an F/A-18 Hornet.

engines still gives a longer range, and the rest is accounted for by the higher percentage of titanium and advanced composite materials used in its construction. As originally designed the F-4 was built with more titanium than any previous fighter, but even in its later versions this only amounted to some 9 per cent by weight of the total structure, whereas the Eagle airframe includes 25.8 per cent titanium, only 5.5 per cent steel and 37.3 per cent aluminium.

The titanium is largely concentrated around the engines and the inboard sections of the wings. The fuselage itself is of conventional semi-monocoque construction, and its pod and twin boom configuration is apparent in the contours of the upper surfaces. The frames of the central pod and of the air intakes on either side and their skin are of machined aluminium, as is the front wing spar, but the three main wing spars and the bulkheads connecting them and the frames of the engine pods are of titanium, also machined. Aft of the forward main wing spar the fuselage skin is also of titanium, and the same metal forms the cantilever booms outboard of each engine which carry the twin fins and horizontal stabilators, the stabilator attachments and the spars of the fins.

Titanium strength

There are several advantages to the use of titanium in these areas. The resulting structure is strong enough to transmit the control forces from the tail surfaces, and the strength of the twin engine bays, with titanium firewalls between them, reduces the risk of a fire or explosion in one engine damaging or incapacitating the other. Similarly, the titanium skin of the inboard underwing skin covers the integral fuel tanks, which are filled with sealant foam injected through channels in the joints between the spars and the aluminium upper skin. Moreover, the titanium wing spars and supporting bulkheads are strong enough to allow the aircraft to keep flying with any one spar in each wing completely severed.

Further weight savings are achieved by the use of composite materials over honeycomb cores for the wing flaps and ailerons and the tailfins and stabilators. The central sections of the tail surfaces, where the titanium structural members form torque boxes, as well as the rudders, are covered with boron composite skins with aluminium and Nomex honeycomb between, while aluminium skins cover the honeycomb flaps and ailerons and the raked outboard sections of the wings. The speedbrake, similarly, has a graphite composite skin

Below: The bubble canopy is the only external feature of the Eagle to interrupt the aerodynamically clean contours of the airframe.

Above: Major structural assemblies of the F-15 airframe. Tail surfaces and wings are interchangeable between aircraft.

Top: Automatic drilling machines in action, forming the attachment holes around the edges of the acrylic windshield destined for an F-15.

over a core of aluminium honeycomb.

The wing torque box assembly is based on the three titanium spars, extended by aft and outer spars of aluminium, and the wings are attached to the titanium bulkheads by pin joints which allow interchangeability between aircraft. The flaps and ailerons are similarly interchangeable, as are the windshield, canopy, speedbrake and fibreglass nose radome, while the vertical stabilizers, rudders and stabilators are interchangeable between right and left sides of the aircraft.

The aircraft is constructed in stages, with individual assemblies built up separately and progressively integrated. The main assemblies are the rear, centre and forward fuselage sections, the vertical and horizontal stabilizers and the wings, and various techniques are used in forming the multitude of sub-assemblies involved.

Sheet aluminium parts are drilled and routed automatically, with more sub-

stantial aluminium sections formed in a two-storey press exerting a pressure of 7,000 tons. Titanium forgings are also finished by computer-controlled milling machinery, and titanium sheets are formed in a furnace at temperatures of 1,650deg F (900deg C) and pressures of 250psi (45kg/sq cm). Graphite skins for the speedbrake are shaped by a high-speed laser cutter, while the honeycomb core is mechanically carved to match. Other automated processes include computerized pipe bending and robot drilling of the attachment holes for the acrylic windshield.

Meanwhile, sheets of the boron epoxy composites used for the tail surfaces are assembled by hand before being bonded by high-pressure steam in an autoclave. Metallic parts are spray-painted individually to protect them from corrosion, and critical subassemblies such as the engine intake ducts and wing leading edges are drilled and riveted by hand. Another job for

Above: Ground crew work under floodlights to prepare a 49th TFW F-15A for a sortie during Red Flag exercises at Nellis AFB in 1980.

Below: A ground crewman sporting an 'Eagle Keeper' badge takes advantage of the ready accessibility of the F-15's internal systems.

skilled technicians is the assembly of the 290 bundles of electric wiring: these are installed during the build-up of the fuselage sections, as are fuel and hydraulic systems.

The final assembly stage brings together the three fuselage sections and the wings, and the final connections of all the power, control and environmental systems. These are checked before the final stage, which involves the installation of engines and avionics, and after a final checkout the aircraft is flown by a company test pilot to ensure that all systems are functioning.

As well as the parts fabricated in MCAIR's own plant, the F-15 involves the use of parts supplied by some 1,200 sub-contractors whose value is approximately half that of the total aircraft cost. By 1980 total cost of the F-15 programme had amounted to $16.58 billion, giving an average unit cost for the 749 aircraft involved of rather more than $22 million (in FY 1980 dollars). The 60 F-15s sold to Saudi Arabia cost a total of $1.92 billion, while Israel's first 40 Eagles were worth $907 million.

Design rationale

The wing configuration is relatively straightforward, though it was only selected after several hundred had been analysed and more than 100 were tested in almost a year of solid wind-tunnel trials. Ultimately, variable camber, with movable surfaces on both leading and trailing edges as used on the F-16, was rejected, since an alternative design with a fixed leading edge employing conical camber was found to offer only slightly higher supersonic drag and marginally reduced subsonic performance, both of which were more than offset by advantages in terms of

weight, simplicity of manufacture and ease of maintenance. The chosen design has a straight leading edge swept at an angle of 45deg, an aspect ratio of 3, zero incidence and 1deg of anhedral.

As outlined in the previous chapter the wingtips were modified from their original shape, a total of 3sq ft (0.28sq m) being removed from each tip to reduce excessive lift at the wingtips and consequent severe buffeting at high g loads and high subsonic speed at altitudes of 30,000ft (9,000m) or so. Another change made as a result of flight testing was the increase in chord of the outer portions of the horizontal stabilators, creating the characteristic notched leading edges of these surfaces, to eliminate flutter. At the same time, the original speedbrake was increased in size by more than 50 per cent, again to eliminate a buffet problem.

Overall, the F-15 profile is designed to minimize wave drag at high speeds, with the single exception of the bubble canopy, which is a feature of both the Eagle and the USAF's other new fighter, the F-16 Fighting Falcon. The aerodynamic penalties imposed by such a canopy are regarded as unavoidable if the pilot is to be enabled to perform his air superiority mission effectively.

The canopy itself is a single transparency with only one transverse frame, hinged at the rear and counterbalanced by a single strut, with a second strut immediately behind the pilot's seat for emergency jettison of the canopy. The size of the canopy is the only external difference between single-seat and two-seat Eagles: the latter have a longer canopy to accommodate the rear crew member, while the single-seater has an avionics bay behind the pilot's seat. This

Left: An F-15B from Nellis AFB's 57th TTW in its hangar for routine servicing during a Red Flag desert warfare simulation.

Right: For maximum maintainability the F-15 airframe features a total of 570sq ft (53sq m) of access doors and panels, as demonstrated here.

houses several avionics 'black boxes' associated with the Tactical Electronic Warfare System in current models but is largely empty and offers ample room for additional avionic equipment; it is unpressurized, and when the canopy is lowered it is isolated by an integral seal.

Directly behind the avionics bay are the fuselage fuel tanks, and between the forward and aft tanks, below the speedbrake, are the ammunition drum and feed system for the M61 cannon. The gun itself is housed in the starboard wing root fairing, while the equivalent fairing at the port wing root contains the flight refuelling receptacle.

The only examples of variable geometry in the F-15's structure are the engine air inlets on either side of the forward fuselage. Because the aircraft was designed to be flown at high angles

Right: Extending steps built into the fuselage side of the F-15 can be used instead of the normal ladder for cockpit access.

of attack in combat, the intakes are able to 'nod' up or down to keep the aperture facing directly into the airflow in order to maintain an adequate supply of air to the engines. The intakes are pivoted at their lower edge and adjusted to angles of 4deg above or 11deg below the horizontal by hydraulic actuators controlled by the air data computer. The intake angle can also be adjusted to prevent more air than necessary being

Below: An 8th TFW Eagle is given an automatic wash at Kwang Ju air base in Korea, during Exercise Cope North in June 1982.

Left: The remarkable slenderness of the F-15's twin vertical tails is achieved by the use of boron composite skins on honeycomb cores.

Above: This manufacturer's drawing of an F-15A shows the layout of the principal systems. No fuel is carried in the wings outboard of the titanium spars and skin.

Right: Wing leading and trailing edge tanks, and additional tanks in the centre fuselage, allow the F-15C to carry an extra 1,855lb (880kg) of fuel internally.

taken in, and the intake surfaces have a further function in providing additional manoeuvring control in a similar manner to canard foreplanes. At supersonic speeds their effectiveness is almost a third as great as that of the stabilators, whose size and weight were enabled to be reduced in consequence. Immediately aft of the intakes themselves are twin mechanically linked ramps to control the shockwaves created in the incoming air.

Of course, structural and aerodynamic efficiency are prerequisites in any aircraft, but a combat aircraft must also be designed to survive the inevitable wear and tear of battle. In this respect the Eagle's main assets are reckoned to be its overall superiority in such areas as pilot visibility, radar detection ability, weapons systems and performance, but a number of less obvious safety features were included, largely as a result of experience with the F-4 in Vietnam, in addition to the basic structural elements described above.

Hydraulics and fuel

As well as twin engines, the F-15 has three separate hydraulic systems which can detect and isolate leaks in their associated subsystems and each of which is capable of sustaining the flight control system on its own. Similarly, twin electrical systems, powered by 40/50kVA AC generators operating through DC conversion units, are capable independently of fulfilling the aircraft's power requirements, while a standby hydraulic generator is fitted to supply critical systems in an emergency. Either the electronic control augmentation system or the hydromechanical system can provide independent flight control should one or the other be put out of action.

Fuel supply is another vital system, and this too is designed to cope with

various emergencies. The fuel tanks themselves are filled with foam, and the fuel lines are also self-sealing. In the event of electrical failure, the fuel system will continue to operate on standby power, providing fuel flow adequate for engine operation up to the mid-afterburner range.

Additional protection against fire is provided in the form of a fire-suppression system. A pressurized bottle containing a non-corrosive agent is located between the engine bay firewalls, with three nozzles able to release the agent into either engine or in the space between them. The provision of this fire suppression system is one of the direct results of the F-4's experiences in Vietnam, and the Eagle is one of the few fighter aircraft to be fitted with such equipment. The physical separation of the fuel tanks from the engine bays is another precaution against fire.

Another aspect of the F-15 design

intended to maximize its efficiency in combat is the emphasis placed on ease of maintenance and relative independence of ground support equipment. The airframe features a total of 570sq ft (53sq m) of access panels, allowing most routine maintenance to be carried out without the use of work stands. The overall simplicity of the airframe is a major factor in reducing maintenance requirements: by comparison with the F-4E, the F-15 has only 202 lubrication points against the earlier fighter's 510; seven hydraulic filters, all of which are interchangeable and which incorporate visual indications of the need for replacement, are used in place of the Phantom's 21; plumbing connections in the fuel system are reduced from 281 to only 97, and the interchangeable fuel pumps are of a plug-in design that allows them to be changed in only 30 minutes; and whereas the F-4E had 905 potted electrical connectors, whose

waterproof compounds were subject to deterioration, the F-15 has a total of 809 silicone grommet connectors to avoid this problem.

The digital avionic systems used also help to reduce the maintenance workload. No routine servicing is needed for these: they are line replaceable units (LRUs), readily removable in the event of failure for testing and repair, and faulty units can be located by means of a built-in test panel located in the nose-wheel well. The cockpit is also equipped with a caution light panel to indicate system failures and a built-in test (BIT) panel for the avionic systems. To reduce dependence on support equipment the secondary power system which provides power for the jet fuel starters can also power the electrical and hydraulic systems for up to 30 minutes while maintenance work is carried out or for munitions loading.

Power for the electrical generators

Left: The separation of the engine bays, with titanium firewalls between, has contributed to the F-15's excellent safety record.

Above: Manufacturer's drawing showing the layout of the principal systems of the F-15C, including engines, fuel, avionics, armament and the dual flight control system.

Left: The increased maximum takeoff weight of the F-15C necessitated strengthening of the undercarriage, tyres and brakes. A 36th TFW F-15C shows its landing gear.

and hydraulic pumps is derived from the main powerplant via an aircraft-mounted accessory drive shaft. Being mounted on the aircraft rather than in the engines themselves, this allows the engines to be interchangeable between right and left. To simplify engine maintenance, each F100 turbofan can be broken down into five main modules, consisting of the inlet and fan, the gearbox, the fan drive, the engine core and the augmentor (afterburner) duct and nozzle. Any of these can be removed for maintenance while another module is substituted, so that a malfunction in one part of the engine does not put the whole powerplant out of action while it is repaired. The engines themselves are removed quickly and easily, sliding out of the rear of the bays on integral rails onto a cart with matching rails, and with only ten disconnections necessary before removal. Complete engine change can be accomplished well

inside the 30 minutes minimum specified by the Air Force. And with the engines installed internal inspections can be carried out by means of 12 borescope ports on each engine.

The overall intention behind this careful planning of maintenance features was to meet a USAF requirement for a maximum of 11.3 maintenance man-hours per flight hour (MMH/FH), just under half the requirement of the F-4E, which would allow a 15 per cent reduction in the number of maintenance personnel. In practice, however, this figure has not been achieved: reduced to 19 by the time type testing was complete, the MMH/FH figure had risen to around 35 by 1980. One reason for this was the continuing difficulties with the engine, as described in the following chapter, with the powerplant absorbing nearly half the total maintenance effort. Another was the continuing shortage of skilled maintenance personnel, partly

as a result of the comparatively low rates of pay which such personnel received compared with those available elsewhere.

An equally serious problem was the difficulties encountered with the Avionics Intermediate Shops (AIS), the second of three stages in the F-15 planned maintenance programme. The first level of maintenance takes place on the flight line, where routine servicing is carried out and line-replaceable units are removed as necessary. The second stage, of which the AIS forms part, is the repair on base of faulty units, and the third is depot repair at Air Logistic Centres.

Among the problems encountered with this system was the difficulty of repairing LRUs on base, with nearly half of the avionics LRUs being returned to the depots. This in turn meant that stocks of replacement LRUs were quickly exhausted. The principal reason

for this state of affairs was the repeated failures of the automated testing stations which comprise the AIS, to the extent that only half the AISs were operational at any time. And the problem was compounded by the failure of the AIS to agree in its diagnosis of the fault with the indications of the on-board BIT equipment in a large percentage of cases.

The natural consequence of all these problems was a high rate of cannibalization, with parts being removed from one aircraft to keep another flying. Consequently, by 1979 availability of the F-15 within TAC had fallen to an alarmingly low 56 per cent. On the other hand, a high degree of readiness has been achieved on numerous exercises, and the Eagle has compiled an impressive safety record. Overall availability by 1983 had risen to more than 65 per cent, and an official inspection of the 1st TFW at Langley in August 1982 found a record 98.6 per cent of aircraft operational: this compares with an availability of only 35 per cent of the same wing's aircraft three years earlier.

New model

Meanwhile, the original F-15A and B production models were replaced by the improved C and D from June 1979. Again, external differences between the single and two-seat version are limited to the slightly longer canopy fitted to the F-15D, and the principal external distinguishing feature of the later models is the provision of the FAST Pack conformal fuel tanks.

The FAST Packs are attached to the outside of each air intake, and can carry an additional 4,875lb (2,211kg) of fuel. Alternatively, sensors such as reconnaissance cameras or infra-red equipment, radar warning receivers and jammers, laser designators and low-light TV cameras, or a combination of such sensors with reduced quantities of fuel, can be carried. When the FAST Packs are fitted, the four Sparrow missiles are mounted on their corners, and bombs or air-to-surface missiles weighing up to 4,400lb (1,995kg) can be carried as an alternative.

Internal fuel capacity of the F-15C/D is also increased by 1,855lb (880kg), with additional tanks located in the centre fuselage and in the wing leading and trailing edges. The effect of this increased fuel capacity is to raise the potential gross weight of the F-15C to 68,000lb (30,845kg) with full internal fuel, FAST Packs and three external tanks. As a result, tyres, wheels and brakes have been strengthened to cope with the increased weight.

The FAST Packs alone carry slightly less fuel than the normal three external tanks, but allow the aircraft to be flown at considerably higher speeds. Compared with the clean configuration, an F-15 equipped with FAST Packs experiences only slightly increased profile drag at subsonic speeds, and compared with the standard external tanks the conformal tanks contribute only a fraction of the former's drag at supersonic speeds. Ferry range with the increased internal fuel, FAST Packs and wing and fuselage tanks is increased to 3,450 miles (5,560km). According to the manufacturers, unused space in the outboard sections of the wings could accommodate a further 900lb (400kg) of fuel.

The manufacturers have also proposed to exploit currently unused internal space, particularly in the rear of the cockpit and in the tail booms, to equip the Eagle for other roles. As much as 56cu ft (1.6cu m) of growth space is claimed to be available for additional avionics, and in the Strike Eagle/Advanced Fighter Capability Demonstrator version of what was originally the second development F-15B the company has already installed a weapon system operator's station in the rear cockpit. Other roles envisaged for developed versions of the Eagle include specialized reconnaissance and Wild Weasel defence suppression models.

The latter would be intended to replace, respectively, the RF-4C and F-4G versions of the aging Phantom, though USAF evaluations during 1983 were concentrated on the dual-role fighter/ground attack role, for which the Eagle was subjected to comparative trials with the F-16XL.

McDonnell Douglas F-15C Eagle cutaway drawing key

1 Tailplane honeycomb construction
2 Boron fibre skin panel
3 Tailplane spars
4 All-moving tailplane pivot fixing.
5 Leading edge dog-tooth
6 Low-voltage formation lighting strip
7 Fin root attachment frames
8 Rudder hydraulic rotary actuator
9 Rudder honeycomb construction
10 Fin spar construction
11 Boron fibre skin panel
12 Anti-collision light
13 Electronic countermeasures aerials (ECM)
14 Variable area afterburner exhaust nozzles
15 Nozzle sealing flaps

16 Fueldraulic nozzle actuators
17 Afterburner duct
18 Engine bay titanium ring frames
19 Rear engine mounting frame
20 Engine bay titanium frame and stringer construction
21 Titanium skin panelling
22 Port tailplane hydraulic actuator
23 Tailplane hinge arm
24 Port rudder
25 Tailboom fairing
26 ECM aerial
27 Port tailplane
28 Tail navigation light
29 ECM aerial
30 Radar warning aerials
31 Boron fibre skin panelling
32 Fin leading edge
33 Port air system equipment bay
34 Forward engine mounting
35 Engine mounting frame
36 Bleed air system ducting
37 Engine support link
38 Engine bay fireproof bulkhead
39 Pratt & Whitney F100-PW-100 afterburning turbofan engine
40 Starboard air system equipment bay
41 Engine bleed air primary heat exchanger
42 Heat exchanger ventral exhaust duct
43 Retractable runway arrester hook
44 Wing trailing edge fuel tank
45 Flap hydraulic jack
46 Starboard plain flap
47 Flap and aileron honeycomb panel construction
48 Starboard aileron
49 Aileron hydraulic actuator
50 Fuel jettison pipe
51 Aluminium honeycomb wing tip fairing
52 Low-voltage formation lighting
53 Starboard navigation light
54 ECM aerial
55 Westinghouse ECM equipment pod
56 Outboard wing stores pylon
57 Pylon attachment spigot
58 Cambered leading edge ribs
59 Front spar
60 Machined wing skin/stringer panels

61 Outboard pylon fixing
62 HF flush aerial
63 Leading edge fuel tank
64 Inboard pylon fixing
65 Wing rib construction
66 Starboard wing integral fuel tank, total internal fuel load, 13,455lb (6103kg)
67 Wing root rib support struts
68 Titanium wing spars
69 Wing spar/fuselage attachment pin joints
70 Machined fuselage main bulkheads
71 Wing/fuselage fuel tank interconnections
72 Airframe mounted engine accessory gearbox
73 Standby hydraulic generator
74 Jet fuel starter (JFS)/auxiliary power unit (APU)
75 Engine intake compressor face

76 Cooling system intake bleed air spill duct
77 Port wing trailing edge fuel tank
78 Port plain flap
79 Flap hydraulic jack
80 Aileron control rod
81 Aileron hydraulic actuator

82 Port aileron
83 Fuel jettison pipe
84 Wing tip fairing
85 Low-voltage formation lighting
86 Port navigation light

102 Intake ducting
103 Ammunition feed chute
104 M61A-1 Vulcan 20mm cannon
105 Hydraulic rotary cannon drive unit
106 Starboard anti-collision light
107 Ventral main undercarriage wheel bay
108 Main undercarriage leg strut
109 Starboard mainwheel
110 Inboard stores pylon
111 Air-to-air missile adaptor
112 Bomb rack
113 Mk 82 low drag 500lb (227kg) HE bombs
114 Bomb triple ejector rack
115 Missile launch rail
116 AIM-9L Sidewinder air-to-air missile

121 Central ammunition drum, 940 rounds
122 Airbrake hinges
123 Forward fuselage fuel tanks
124 UHF aerial
125 Intake duct bleed air louvres
126 Intake bypass air spill duct
127 Variable area intake ramp hydraulic actuator
128 Air conditioning system cooling air exhaust duct
129 Canopy hinge point
130 Air conditioning plant
131 Intake incidence control jack
132 Intake duct variable area ramp doors
133 Intake pivot fixing
134 Starboard engine air intake
135 Nosewheel leg door
136 Nose undercarriage leg strut
137 Nosewheel
138 Landing/taxying lamps
139 Nosewheel retraction strut
140 Rear underfloor equipment bay
141 Tactical electronic warfare system (TEWS) racks

147 Cockpit aft decking
148 Canopy arch
149 Port intake external compression lip
150 Fuel and sensor tactical (FAST) pack, conformal fuel pallet, capacity 5,000lb (2268kg)
151 600US gal (2270 litre) external fuel tank
152 Cockpit canopy cover
153 Ejection seat headrest
154 Seat safety handle/arming lever
155 Canopy emergency jettison linkage
156 Ejection seat launch rails
157 Safety harness
158 McDonnell Douglas ACES II "zero-zero" ejection seat
159 Cockpit sloping bulkhead
160 Pilots side console panel
161 Air conditioning ducting
162 Forward underfloor equipment bay, built-in test equipment (BITE) and liquid oxygen converter
163 Low-voltage formation lighting strip
164 Port side retractable boarding ladder
165 TACAN aerial
166 Angle of attack probe
167 Rudder pedals

Above left: With its paint removed the Streak Eagle clearly shows the boron composite skins of its rudder and vertical stabilizer.

Above: Control surfaces of the F-15 are limited to wing flaps and ailerons, twin rudders and all-moving horizontal stabilators.

ACES II ejection seat

A Environmental sensor pitots
B Recovery parachute container
C FLCS data recorder
D Recovery parachute risers
E Emergency oxygen bottle
F Emergency oxygen pressure gauge
G Inertia reel knob
H Ejection control safety lever
I Radio beacon switch
J Survival kit (under seat pan)
K Ejection handle
L Restraint emergency release handle
M Lap belt and survival kit attachment
N Emergency oxygen fitting

168 Control column
169 Pilot's head-up display (HUD)
170 Instrument panel shroud
171 Frameless windscreen panel
172 ADF sense aerial
173 Radio and electronics equipment bay, port and starboard
174 Cockpit front pressure bulkhead
175 Pitot tube
176 UHF aerial
177 Radar mounting bulkhead
178 Radome hinge mounting
179 ILS aerial
180 Radar scanner mounting and tracking mechanism
181 Hughes APG-63 pulse doppler radar scanner
182 Scanner mounted IFF aerial array
183 Glass-fibre radome

87 ECM aerial
88 Cambered leading edge
89 Outboard pylon fixing
90 Port wing internal fuel tank
91 Fuel system piping
92 Inboard pylon fixing
93 Leading edge fuel tank
94 Anti-collision light
95 Boom-type air refuelling receptacle
96 Bleed air duct to air conditioning plant
97 Control rod runs
98 Dorsal airbrake, open
99 Airbrake glass-fibre honeycomb construction
100 Airbrake hydraulic jack
101 Centre fuselage fuel tanks

117 AIM-7F Sparrow air-to-air missile
118 Sparrow missile launcher unit
119 Cannon muzzle aperture
120 Cannon barrels

142 Cockpit coaming
143 Rear pressure bulkhead
144 Canopy jack
145 Cockpit pressurization valves
146 Structural space provision for second crew member (F-15D)

Above: The McDonnell Douglas ACES II ejection seat as fitted to the F-15. At zero airspeed the catapult ignites within 0.3sec, followed by the rocket sustainer in 0.45sec, separation of pilot from the seat after 1.3sec, opening of the parachute pack in 2.3sec and full inflation of the parachute in about 5sec.

Powerplant

A fighter pilot needs as much power as he can get, so a fighter designed to be the best in the world needs most power of all. The thrust demanded for the F-15 pushed US engine technology to its limits, and the F100 turbofan has had its share of problems. But when a principal source of engine wear turns out to be pilots flying aircraft in ways that were never possible before the manufacturers have reason to congratulate themselves. Meanwhile, the F100 has formed the basis for newer powerplants, and there are new engines under development as possible replacements in a new generation of Eagles.

Development of the Pratt & Whitney F100 turbofan started in August 1968, when the USAF awarded development contracts to P&W and General Electric for engines suitable for use in the planned FX fighter. In view of the high thrust-to-weight ratio planned for the new fighter, the resulting engines would have to push the technology of the time to its limits. P&W faced the daunting task of developing a powerplant producing 25 per cent more thrust per unit of weight than the then-current TF30 turbofan used in the F-111, and twice that of the J75 turbojet used in the F-105 Thunderchief and F-106 Delta Dart.

Both companies built and ran demonstration engines whose light weight, high thrust and low fuel consumption were well in advance of previous designs. The P&W engine was selected by the USAF for further development, contracts being awarded in 1970. Two versions were originally planned – the F100 for the USAF and the F401, intended to power later models of the US Navy's

Below: An F-15A of the 32nd TFS, its engines in full afterburner, accelerates down the runway at Camp New Amsterdam.

F-14 Tomcat, but the latter was cancelled when the USN was ordered by the Department of Defense to cut back the size of the planned F-14 fleet.

The F100 is an axial-flow turbofan with a bypass ratio of 0.7:1. It has two shafts – one carrying a three-stage fan driven by a two-stage turbine, the other carrying the ten-stage main compressor and its two-stage turbine. The completed engine is 191in (4.85m) long and 34.8in (0.88m) in diameter at the inlet, and weighs 3,068lb (1,391kg).

Powder metallurgy

New technologies used in the F100 included powder metallurgy. Instead of forming some metal components in the traditional manner, P&W reduced the raw material to a powder. This could be heated and formed under high pressure to create engine components better able to tolerate the high temperatures planned for the F100 core.

Operating temperature of the F100 turbine was far above that of earlier engines. Successful turbojets of earlier vintage, such as the GE F85 which powers the F-5E, or the GE J79 used in the F-4 and F-104, had turbine inlet temperatures of around 1,800deg F

(982deg C). P&W had achieved figures of just over 2,000deg F (1,093 deg C) in the TF30 turbofan, but to meet the demanding requirements of the F100 specification involved temperatures of 2,565deg F (1,407deg C).

Use of such advanced technology resulted in an engine capable of providing the high levels of thrust required. Maximum thrust is normally described as being 'in the 15,000lb (6,800kg) thrust class' when running without afterburner, and 'in the 25,000lb (11,340kg) class' when full augmentation is selected.

Normal dry (non-afterburning) rating is 12,420lb (5,634kg), rising to a maximum of 14,670lb (6,654kg) at full Military Intermediate rating – the maximum attainable without afterburning. Specific fuel consumption (sfc) – the amount of thrust produced for each pound of fuel burned per hour – is 0.69 at normal rating and 0.71 at Military Intermediate. At full afterburning power, the F100 develops 23,830lb (10,809kg) of thrust at an sfc of 2.17. At this rating, the engine swallows an impressive 860lb (390kg) of fuel per minute.

By the time the F-15 was ready for its first flight in July 1972, the F100 had

Above: The convergent/divergent nozzles of an F-15's twin Pratt & Whitney F100s fully open in the afterburning position.

completed most of its test programme, meeting 23 out of 24 critical 'project milestones'. Between February and October of the following year, a series of turbine failures dogged attempts to complete the 150-hour running trial which formed part of the formal Qualification test. The latter was the most punishing series of tests to which any US military jet engine had ever been subjected, according to P&W. It included 30 hours of running at a simulated speed of Mach 2.3, and 38 hours of running at a simulated Mach 1.6.

Following completion of this test, the F100 was subjected to a further series of intensive trials, including 150 hours of running at over-temperature conditions, and a long series of accelerated Mission Tests. Conducted on the ground, but designed to simulate the stresses of operational service, these were intended to build up running time and detect potential problems. The latter were not serious enough to delay the start of production. The powerplant is

1	3-stage fan	5	2-stage fan-drive turbine
2	Smokeless annular combustor	6	2-stage compressor-drive turbine
3	Variable convergent/divergent nozzle	7	10-stage compressor
4	Augmentor		

Above: Evolution of the afterburning turbofan (bottom) via the turbojet (top), afterburning turbojet and straight turbofan.

Above: Factory inspection of an F100. The engine weighs 3,068lb (1,391kg) and has a thrust-to-weight ratio of nearly 8:1 at full augmentation.

Above: Comparison of the thrust available per inch of engine length from powerplants of (left to right) the F-15, F-111F, F-4E and F-5E.

Top: Exterior of the F100, with diagram of its principal components. Nearly half its length is occupied by the augmentor chamber and nozzle.

designated F100-PW-100 by the company and JTF22A-25A by the USAF.

USAF hopes that the F100 would be a fully-reliable powerplant by the time the F-15 entered service were confounded by a series of technical and operational problems. Strikes at two major subcontractors delayed the delivery of engines, while service experience showed that the F100 was wearing out twice as fast as had been predicted. By the end of 1979 the USAF was being forced to accept engineless F-15 airframes, and by the spring of the following year around 30 were in storage. A massive effort by P&W brought the delivery situation under control, but for a long time the F-15 fleet remained short of engines.

A modification introduced into the fuel pump of the F100 created problems for the F-15 early in its career. In cruising flight, cavitation could begin in the pump, badly damaging the pump vanes. The solution adopted was simple – revert to the original design. In the case of the single-engined F-16 Fighting Falcon, which also uses the F100, a pump failure would be more serious, so Sunstrand developed an alternative dual-element pump for this aircraft. This runs at a lower speed, and should one section fail, the other can continue to deliver fuel at a lower rate.

The electronic engine control unit uses the fuel as a coolant. This technique for obtaining 'free' cooling led to problems when the F-15 first entered

service. During training missions at Luke AFB, aircraft sometimes had to wait for 45 minutes or more before takeoff, with engines running at idle settings. This gradually heated the mass of fuel in the Eagle's tanks to the point where it was no longer cold enough to cool the engine control unit.

Modified fuel flow
Given the high temperature of the desert environment at Luke, the unit could not radiate the excess heat away, so tended to overheat. This resulted in engine overspeed problems and turbine failures. The fix in this case, according to the Burrows/Shawler paper presented to the Society of Experimental Test Pilots in 1975, was to cut back the fuel flow rate of the electronic engine control, based on the rate of temperature increase, just prior to full military power. Acceleration time was reduced by this modification to less than 50 per cent of the original time.

Another early problem was that the afterburner light-up envelope was considered too restrictive. Among the more important changes was one involving the five-segment afterburner range (practically mandatory for all fan engines) designed to make a smooth transition between segments, where the

Right: Test equipment is positioned on an F100 at Pratt & Whitney's Government Products Division, West Palm Beach, Florida.

main problems were either too rich a mixture causing a light and then a blow-out, or too lean a mixture preventing a relight at all.

The spray-ring of each segment of the afterburner has a quick-fill capability which controls the light-up of each segment. The amount of fuel in each segment was the same for all altitudes and speeds, resulting in insufficient fuel at sea level and too much at high altitudes. The solution was the provision of a barometric sensor to reduce the amount of fuel fed into the quick-fill area as altitude was increased. The improvement is described as 'the biggest increment' on this problem.

The other major afterburner change

was to reduce fuel flow in full reheat mode, which countered the effects of excess fuel for airflow and afterburner size. By reducing the total fuel flow by a nominal 4,000lb/hr (1,814kg/hr), the blow-out difficulty at full reheat was eliminated. An additional benefit was equal or greater thrust for less fuel flow.

The limited throttle movement came in for some criticism at this stage of the flight testing. Originally, the rpm was to be kept to a minimum at all altitudes, thus allowing 65 per cent rpm at 40,000ft (12,000m). This caused problems in getting the engine out of idle, due to low fuel flow, while requiring a slow throttle movement for acceptable acceleration. The fix was simple enough, involving increasing the idling rpm in line with increasing altitude.

On the air intakes, which incorporate a variable-geometry ramp to adjust the airflow at varying speeds and heights to the optimum required by the engine, months of wind-tunnel research paid off. The amount of travel provided for the ramp was found to be more than necessary, and the engine inlet compatibility testing was completed in four months. Similar testing with the F-4 Phantom took 22 months, and with the F-101 Voodoo some 30 months.

Early operational and durability problems with the F100 during the late 1970s were largely overcome by modifications plus improvements in materials, maintenance and operating procedures. Production of spare parts was accelerated, and field maintenance teams were increased in size.

Part of the problem lay in the fact that the USAF had underestimated the number of cycles which engines aboard such high-performance types as the F-15 and F-16 would actually undergo. (A cycle is defined as the temperature variation experienced in a mission from engine start to maximum power and afterburner, then back to the lower settings used for landing). In 1977 the service estimated that each engine would undergo 1.15 cycles per flight hour. In practice the rate was 2.2 for the F-15 and 3.1 for the F-16.

At one time, designers had assumed that the most arduous duty which a jet engine had to face was running for long periods at high power levels. By the late

1960s, research had shown that this was simply not the case. Many failures were due to this type of running, but others were created by the heating and cooling resulting from an engine being run up to high power then throttled back.

Technicians dubbed this 'low-cycle fatigue', but had to admit that it was difficult to measure. To aid the design of future engines such as the F100, estimates were made of the average number of thermal cycles to which an engine would be exposed per flying hour. Unfortunately for the F100 programme, these estimates were wrong. In practice, engines were being subjected to far more thermal cycles than the designers had allowed for.

Overworked engines

Paradoxically, the additional stress which the engines were receiving was largely due to the F-15 and F-16 being such good aircraft. Given the high manoeuvrability of their new mounts, pilots were flying in a manner not possible on earlier types, pushing the aircraft to high angles of attack and making full use of the extended performance envelope. In the heat of a dogfight, the throttle setting would be changed much more often than on earlier fighters. All this spelled hard work for the engine.

Critical components such as first-stage turbine blades showed signs of

Below: The titanium frames of an F-15 engine bay, with the powerplant about to be installed, as seen by the wide-angle lens.

distress, condemnation rate during repair being 60 per cent instead of the predicted 20 per cent. Maximum gas temperature was reduced to conserve component life, while R&D funding was concentrated on improvements to reliability rather than increasing thrust. Despite these problems, the F-15 had a better engine related safety record by the end of the 1970s than any other USAF fighter at a comparable point in its service career.

Another problem which was to dog the F100 during the first years of its service career was stagnation stalling. The compressor blades in a jet engine are of aerofoil section, and, like the

Above: The split tail of the F-15 allows the stabilators and vertical stabilizers to be kept well clear of the efflux from the engines.

wing of an aircraft, can be stalled if the angle at which the airflow strikes them exceeds a critical value. Powerplant stalls are occasional occurrences in most jet engines, particularly in the early stages of development, and the F100 was to prove excessively vulnerable to stagnation stalling during its first few years of operational service.

Turbofans are prone to a particularly severe type of stall from which recovery is not possible. As the flow of air through the compressor is disturbed, the engine core looses speed, while the combustor section of the engine continues to pass hot gas to the turbine, causing the latter to overheat. If this condition is not noticed, the turbine may be damaged.

Experience with the F-15 showed that in the event of a mild hard start, the pilot might not notice that a stall had occurred, as the loss of acceleration on the twin-engined aircraft was often not sharp enough to indicate to the pilot that one engine had failed. Unless he checked the temperature gauge, low-pressure turbine entry temperature could reach the point were damage might occur. To avoid this problem, an audible-warning system was devised.

Some stagnation stalls were found to be due to component failures, but most were linked with afterburner problems. The latter usually took the form of 'hard starts' – virtually mini-explosions within the afterburner. In some cases the afterburner failed to light on schedule; in other instances the burner extinguished. In either event, large amounts of unburned fuel were sprayed into the jetpipe, creating a momentary build-up of fuel. When this was ignited by the hot efflux from the engine core, a pressure pulse was created – the aerospace equivalent of a car backfiring.

Deliberate hard start

A reporter from the journal *Aviation Week* gave this account of a deliberately-induced hard start on a test stand: "The force of the auto-ignition was sufficient to rock the heavily sound-insulated concrete test building. A large gout of flame at the afterburner exhaust was seen on the closed-circuit color-television system."

The pressure in the afterburner resulting from a hard start sent a shock wave back up through the fan duct. When this reached the front section of the engine, it could cause the fan to stall, the high-pressure compressor to stall, or, in the worst case, both. It was sometimes possible for a series of stagnation stalls to occur, with each resulting in the afterburner hard start needed to trigger off another.

Stagnation stalls usually took place at altitude and at high Mach numbers, but rarely below 20,000ft (6,100m). Normal recovery method was for the pilot to shut down the engine, and allow it to spool down. Once the tachometer showed that engine rpm had fallen below the 50 per cent mark, the throttle could safely be reopened to the idle position, and the F100 would carry out its automatic relight sequence. Critical factor in restarting the engine after a stagnation stall is the low-pressure turbine-inlet temperature. This must fall to 450deg F (232deg C) before the engine can be restarted.

Several modifications were devised to reduce the frequency of stagnation stalls. The first approach taken was to try to prevent pressure build-ups in the afterburner. A quartz window in the side of the afterburner assembly allowed a flame sensor to monitor the pilot flame of the augmentor. If this went out, the flow of fuel to the outer sections of the burner was stopped.

When the F100 engine-control system was originally designed, P&W engineers allowed for the possibility that ingestion of efflux from missiles might stall the engine. A 'rocket fire' facility was designed into the controls in order to cope with such an eventuality. When missiles were fired, an electronic signal could be sent to the unified fuel control system which supplies fuel to the engine core and to the afterburner. The angle of the variable stator blades in the engine could be altered to avoid a stall,

while the fuel flow to the engine was momentarily reduced, and the afterburner exhaust was increased in area to reduce the magnitude of any pressure pulse in the afterburner.

Tests had shown that the 'rocket fire' facility was not needed, but P&W engineers were able to use it as a means of preventing stagnation stalls. Engine shaft speed, turbine temperature and the angle of the compressor stator blades are monitored on the F100 by a digital electronic engine control unit. This normally serves to 'fine-tune' the engine throughout flight to ensure optimum performance.

By monitoring and comparing HP spool speed and fan exhaust temperature, the engine control unit is able to sense that a stagnation stall is about to take place, and send a dummy 'Rocket Fire' signal to the unified fuel control system to initiate the anti-stall measures described above. At the same time, a second modification to the fuel control system reduces the afterburner setting to zone 1 – little more than a pilot light – in order to help reduce pressure within the jetpipe.

In an attempt to prevent any pulses coming forward through the fan duct from affecting the core, P&W engineers devised a modification known as the 'proximate splitter'. This is a forward extension to the internal casing which

Below: Eagles rendezvous with a KC-10A tanker. Specific fuel consumption of the F100 is 2.17 with full augmentation.

splits the incoming airflow coming from the engine compressor fan, passing some to the core of the engine and diverting the remainder down the fan duct, past the core and into the afterburner. By closing the gap between the front end of the fan to just under half an inch (1.3cm), the engine designers reduced the size of the path by which the high-pressure pulses from the burner had been reaching the core.

Engines fitted with the proximate splitter were test-flown in the F-15, but this modification was not embodied in the engines of production Eagles, whose twin engines made the loss of a

Above: The 'nodding' air intakes on either side of the F-15's forward fuselage are necessary to maintain the optimum rate of airflow to the engines, and for operation at high angles of attack.

single engine less hazardous. It was, however, fitted to engines destined for the single-engined F-16.

The improvement in reliability as a result of the modifications to the fuel control system and nozzle was dramatic. Back in 1976, the F-15 fleet experienced a stagnation stall rate of 11–12 per 1,000 flying hours; by the end of 1981 this had dropped to 1.5 per 1,000 hours.

Above: A two-seat F-15 approaches a tanker boom for refuelling. Economical at normal ratings, the F100 consumes 860lb (390kg) of fuel per minute in full afterburner.

Efforts are under way to further reduce the smoke output of the F100 as part of a planned component-improvement programme. For example, the combustor has been modified to increase the velocity of the airflow in its front end, resulting in improved mixing of air and fuel and leading to more complete combustion and less residual smoke.

Traditional engine-servicing techniques involve replacing critical components at the end of a statistically-calculated lifetime. This often results in components being removed and scrapped while still perfectly servicable, giving good safety margins, but at a high cost to the operator. The USAF now wants engine designers to develop

parts with greater tolerance to crack damage so that these may be left in the engine until inspection by non-destructive test (NDT) methods shows that cracks are starting to develop and a replacement is needed. Life-cycle costs may be cut by up to 60 per cent.

The service's Damage Tolerant Design (DTD) programme involved both Pratt & Whitney and General Electric, and focussed much of its attention on the F100. One of the programme's first achievements was a new pattern of F100 fan disc having five times the life of the original component. Key design elements under DTD are high quality control of the raw material, and the avoidance of shapes and configurations such as sharp radii which cause stress concentrations.

The Air Force plans to begin testing engine discs currently under development as part of the DTD programme in 1984, and hopes to fit these into operational engines before the end of that

Below left: The General Electric F110 has been test-flown in an F-15, and is one candidate to power future variants of the Eagle.

Top: The P&W PW1120 is based on the core of the F100: smaller and lighter, it is to be used in the Israel Aircraft Industries Lavi fighter.

Above: The other potential replacement for the F100 is P&W's own PW1128, which began test-flying in March 1983.

year. By 1985 or 1986 the F100 may be fitted with second and third-stage turbine blades and vanes manufactured using a single-crystal technique. Although more expensive than components made from traditional materials, these will probably have a lifetime at least twice that of current vanes and blades.

The USAF was the first F100 user to take advantage of a warranty scheme offered by P&W in 1980. The company undertook to repair or replace certain high-pressure turbines unserviceable as a result of wear or mechanical failure at no extra cost to the USAF. Engines covered by the deal were from production lot IX and were due for delivery between February 1981 and January 1982.

To qualify for free treatment, faulty engines would have to have carried out less than 900 equivalents of the TAC engine operating cycle (about two years of normal use) or develop the fault

within three and a half years of delivery. If the HP failure had caused secondary damage to the engine, P&W undertook to cover costs up to 75 per cent of that of a new engine.

Pratt & Whitney are continuing research into new engines based on the F100 and its technology. During a series of tests carried out in late summer of 1982, the company ground-tested an F100 fitted with a two-dimensional nozzle. Rectangular in cross-section, this is a convergent/divergent design featuring moveable upper and lower surfaces which could be used to vector the thrust. This design was developed under a USAF contract, and while no production applications is planned, the new nozzle could be used in a modified F-16 or F-15.

Angles of up to 20deg were demonstrated, but P&W is confident that the design would be good for up to 30deg. Coupled with the use of thrust reversing, this technique could greatly in-

crease the agility of current aircraft, and could cut the take-off run to 1,200ft (366m) or less. Earlier attempts to design axisymmetric nozzles with vectoring and thrust-reversing have resulted in complex and heavy units which paid a high penalty in thrust loss. The latest P&W design could be offered as an add-on modification, weighing only a few hundred pounds, to the standard F100 gas generator section.

Using experience gained from the F100 programme, P&W was able to begin development of the cropped-fan PW1120 afterburning turbofan. Based on the core of the earlier engine, this is a low-risk development with 60 per cent commonality, but incorporating a new low-pressure compressor and turbine and a simplified afterburner. Operating temperatures have been slightly reduced, and the PW1120 has a slightly lower thrust-to-weight ratio of 7.25:1 instead of 7.9:1. The PW1120 is some 20in (51cm) shorter than the F100 and

7in (18cm) narrower in diameter. It is rated at 20,620lb (9,342kg) and is due to fly early in 1984. The first application of the PW1120 to be announced was the planned Israel Aircraft Industries Lavi air combat fighter.

Two other engines are currently under development, aimed at re-engining the F-15, F-16 and, possibly, the F-14. An up-market version of the F100, variously known as the F100EMD, PW1130 and now the PW1128, has its mass flow increased to 248lb/sec (112.5kg/sec), a turbine entry temperature of 2,700degF (1,482degC) single crystal blades and digital electronic controls. The PW1128 began test-flying in March 1983, with a rating of 26,900lb (12,200kg). Its production rating will be 27,410lb (12,430kg).

Competing with the PW1128 is the General Electric F110 (formerly the F101 DFE – derivative fighter engine) rated at 27,500lb (12,470kg), which has flown in both the F-14 and the F-16XL. Both engines may well be bought, but the split has yet to be determined: one possibility is the installation of the PW1128 in the F-15, and the F110 in the F-14 and F-16.

Avionics

The key to the Eagle's combat capability is its sophisticated suite of avionics: long-range, look-down radar that can detect even low-flying targets at ranges of up to 100 miles (160km); a tactical electronic warfare system to warn of any threat; and displays and controls that present the pilot with almost all the information he needs and allow him to control weapon systems and radar without looking inside the cockpit. The addition of programmable signal processing has further increased the radar capability, and for the ground-attack role still more improvements are planned.

When considering the anatomy of a modern aeroplane the airframe can be likened to the skeleton and flesh, the engines provide muscle and the on-board computers and avionics can be considered as the brain and nervous system. For many years the avionic systems were relatively simple and were purely add-on items to assist in communication and navigation: failure of any one item did not create any great problem, and the aeroplane could fly quite happily under human control and judgement. Then came the great electronic revolution and the emergence of the silicon chip.

The evolution of the integrated circuit – an entire microelectronic system embodied in a chip of semiconductive material, normally crystalline silicon – brought immediate gains to the designers of avionic equipment. The size and weight of 'black boxes' could be drastically reduced; power consumption fell, the associated need for complicated cooling systems; reliability increased; and, perhaps most significantly, the new devices allowed for a considerable expansion of functions.

Computers that had once required large storage space shrank to shoe-box size, offered great reliability and could be programmed for a variety of complex tasks. With programming came the new word 'software', denoting an arcane, subjective art that can achieve the apparently impossible.

Generally, software can be considered as the process of telling a computer what to do and how to do it, while making the process understandable to the computer itself. This last consideration is crucial to efficient operation, since a computer totally lacks judgement and intuition and cannot relate in any useful manner to past experience. Consequently, the software must be able to dictate behaviour under all operating conditions including abnormal situations.

High-speed operation

A major advantage of electronic systems is that they operate at the speed of light, allowing a considerable number of operations to take place in a very short space of time. If a pilot operates a switch which affects a circuit under computer control and at that point the computer is working hard it may introduce a delay of perhaps one tenth of a second. This is a valuable breathing space for the computer, yet so short as to be entirely unnoticeable to the pilot.

As well as operational functions, software programs can be used to carry out automatic test and system monitoring, constantly evaluating the health of the associated hardware and providing an indication of malfunction to the pilot. This is an extremely important part of a modern avionic system, usually referred to as built-in test equipment (BITE). It enables failures to be identified and isolated, allowing the pilot to carry on with the operation by selecting alternate systems. One manufacturer of such equipment is on record as saying that a typical system with 100,000 computer instructions may use almost three quarters of this capacity for diagnostic purposes.

As the electronic revolution gained pace so avionic equipment became more complex. By the early 1970s systems were evolving with considerable computational powers, and with digital computers forming an integral part. Reliability had improved and maintenance had been simplified by the use of self-checking systems. More and more critical functions came under the control of electronic systems and the avionic suite now ranked alongside airframe and engine as an essential and fundamental element. Integration of these three areas has reached the point where it is now inconceivable that any part of a modern military aircraft should not be

Above: The McDonnell Douglas head-up display present all essential navigation and attack information to the Eagle pilot.

under some form of electronic control of influence.

A modern aeroplane such as the F-15 depends upon electronic systems for communication, navigation, flight management, weapons management, automatic flight control (auto-pilot), systems control and management (eg hydraulics and pressurization), control and management of electronic warfare (EW) systems and the continual monitoring of all aspects of engine and airframe operation and maintenance. Indeed, the pace of change in modern technology and military tactics to meet evolving threats is such that any simple list of electronic devices is necessarily incomplete. Although the aeroplane appears externally unchanged, its black boxes can undergo constant evolution and refinement, and the practised eye can sometimes note the addition of certain lumps, bulges and antennas on the external surface of the airframe.

Below: Nose radars, HUDs and bubble canopies give these F-15s unmatched target detection ability.

Air-to-air gun mode

- Master arm 'on' (gun boresight line)
- Aircraft waterline
- Indicated airspeed scale (F-15 at 445kt)
- Aiming reticle (50mil radius; range 1,000ft per spoke)
- Gun armed, 999 rounds left
- Flight path ladder
- Heading scale (120deg indicated)
- Altitude scale (355ft indicated)
- 10-mile radar ranging scale
- Target designator on acquired target
- Target at 2,000ft
- Closing at 150kt
- Discretes
- Velocity vector

Air-to-air medium range missile mode

- Master arm 'on' (gun boresight line)
- Steering circle
- Steering dot
- Indicated airspeed scale (F-15 at 445kt)
- Velocity vector
- Missiles armed, 4 MRMs ready
- Flight path ladder
- Heading scale (120deg indicated)
- Target designator
- 40-mile radar ranging scale
- Altitude scale (355ft indicated)
- Target closing at 950kt at 22 miles
- Target in missile range
- 60sec to missile impact

Air-to-ground automatic mode

- Master arm/gun cross 'on'
- Release cue
- Indicated airspeed scale (reading 450kt)
- Azimuth steering line
- Pitch scale
- Heading scale (360deg indicated)
- Altitude scale (5,000ft indicated)
- Air-to-ground reticle (10,000ft range indicated)
- Target designator
- Time-to-go
- Pull-up cue

Air-to-ground CDIP mode

- Master arm/gun cross 'on'
- Indicated airspeed scale (reading 450kt)
- Pull-up cue
- Pitch scale
- Heading scale (360deg indicated)
- Velocity vector
- Altitude scale (5,000ft indicated)
- Target designator
- Displayed impact line
- Air-to-ground reticle (6,900ft range indicated)

Above: Typical displays presented by the F-15 HUD showing the symbology used in various air-to-air and air-to-ground attack modes.

This is an important aspect of avionic innovation as it can enhance abilities and performance even though the aircraft is still restricted by its own basic dynamic performance. In other words, the power/weight ratio tends to remain constant, but its electronic eyes and brain can become more far-seeing and powerful so that it can be a more effective fighting machine.

The basic electrical power of the F-15 is provided by engine driven generators manufactured by the Lear Siegler Power Equipment Division. These feature a 40/50kVA generator constant speed drive unit, produced by the Sundstrand Corporation, which ensures that the generator itself is always driven at a constant speed regardless of engine speed or revolutions. This in turn ensures a constant, steady output of closely controlled electrical power in terms of voltage, frequency and phase and does away with the need for additional on-board devices to ensure such

basic integrity of power supplies. Power is then distributed throughout the aircraft via other control systems, circuit breakers, distribution boards and transformer-rectifiers to ensure adequate power, of the correct type, for each sequence of operation. For instance, certain switched selection circuits can accept fairly brutal power sources while other types of instrumentation require highly accurate and sensitive power inputs.

Much of the flight information can be presented to the pilot on a cathode ray tube (CRT) display, which can accept

inputs from radar or electro-optical sensors. This is in line with the current trend for information to be presented in visual terms, often supported by colour. The pilot can assimilate more information more efficiently and ambiguity is reduced. An IBM on-board digital air data computer is used to process information from other sensors such as al-

Below: View through the head-up display following the launch of a medium-range AIM-7 Sparrow. The missile itself is visible in the target designator box.

Left: The front panel of the F-15C cockpit has all the most frequently used controls conveniently mounted and a minimum of instruments.

1 Microphone switch
2 IFF interrogate button
3 Target designate control
4 Gunsight reticle stiffen/reject short-range missile
5 Radar antenna elevation control
6 ECM dispenser switch
7 Weapon selection switch (gun, short-range missile or medium-range missile)
8 Spare
9 Speed brake switch

1 Trim button
2 Weapon release button
3 Radar auto acquisition switch
4 Autopilot/nose gear steering release switch
5 SRM/EO weapon seeker head cage/uncage control
6 HUD camera and gun trigger

Above: The throttles (top) and control stick carry all the weapons and radar controls needed in combat, enabling the pilot to keep his eyes attention on the target or HUD.

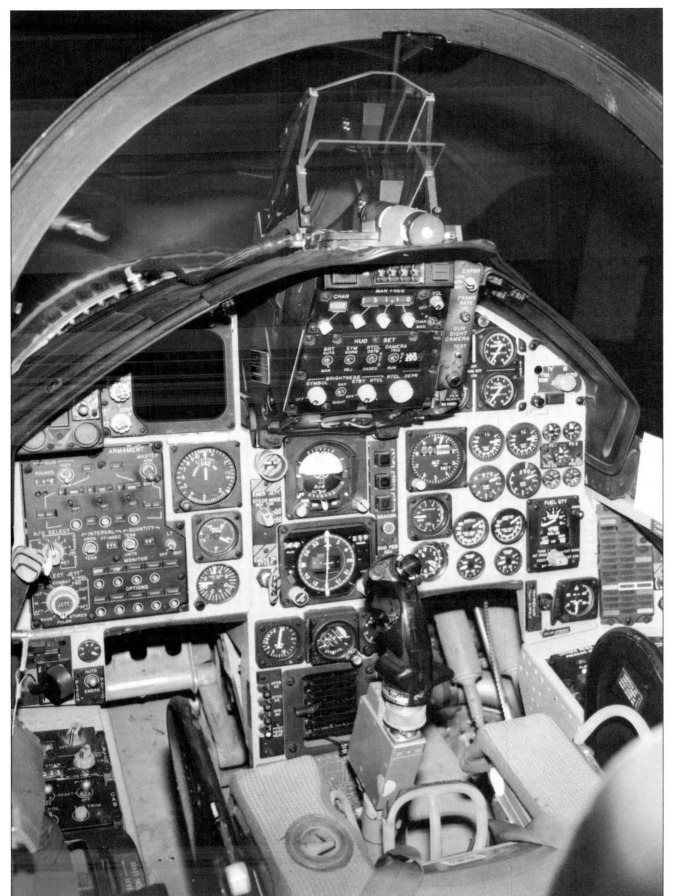

timeters, and this too is presented on the CRT display.

Communication is usually through VHF/UHF links, which essentially form a line-of-sight system. In other words, the range of the equipment is directly proportional to the aircraft's height above the ground. For long-distance flights, therefore, the communications system is supplemented by HF to provide the necessary range. Interference by the enemy is always a problem in communications and several programmes have been undertaken to overcome the problem. Typically, the signal can be spread over a wide spectrum to reduce the chances of detection and require a widely spread jamming signal with consequent dissipation of power and loss of effectiveness.

The aircraft's Litton ASN-109 navigation system is based upon inertial navigation techniques. This is a completely passive, on-board system which does not have to rely on ground-based aids and is largely automatic in operation. It depends upon highly sensitive gyroscopes which are used to accurately align a platform in relation to true North. The pilot tells the computer the start point and can add several desired destinations or waypoints, and as the aircraft moves off, accelerometers on the platform detect rates of movement. All the information is then processed by a digital computer, which comes up with a variety of answers which are displayed to the pilot. This information includes position, time to go to next waypoint and wind conditions.

The high degree of accuracy of platform stabilization can give attitude information for the aircraft's flight instruments providing pitch, roll and heading data at all times. This navigation system is backed up by ground-based navaids such as TACAN, ADF and ILS allowing the F-15 to integrate with any type of traffic pattern. In a cross-country mode these aids can be used to update the inertial system.

Among the most classified equipment is that concerned with aspects of electronic warfare (EW). This is also likely to be the system most often modified, changed and reprogrammed. EW systems can be used to detect radars, notify the pilot of various types of hostile EW and allow a degree of offensive reaction such as jamming enemy signals. Such is the state of modern electronics that many of these devices act completely automatically and can recognize the difference between friendly and hostile emissions. They are capable of reacting to rapid changes in the enemy scenario and can fire off decoys such as chaff or infra-red (IR) flares to confuse the seeker of enemy missiles.

The F-15 carries such a system in the Northrop ALQ-135, which is part of the aircraft's tactical electronic warfare system (TEWS) and is associated with the active jamming role.

More readily apparent is the Loral ALR-56 radar warning receiver, four external antennas mounted at each wing tip and on top of each fin give them a distinctive, easily recognizable shape. A fifth blade-shaped antenna is mounted under the forward fuselage. Associated equipment includes receivers, power supply, receiver controls and a display of an alpha-numeric type which indicates the degree of lethality and range of the emerging threat. The all-solid-state ALR-56 is based on a digitally controlled dual channel receiver which scans from H-band through to J-band (6-20GHz), while changes in the perceived threat can be accommodated by changes in software.

The APG-63 radar

While it is invidious to suggest that any one part of the avionic system is more important than any other in these days of integrated and interrelated systems, it is hard not to admit that the awesome capability of the Hughes APG-63 radar is really the heart of the F-15 and the

EMERGENCY
AIR REFUELING
HANDLE

BIT PANEL

IFF

RADAR

FUEL

COMMUNICATIONS

EXTERIOR LIGHTS

THROTTLE
QUADRANT

CONTROL
AUGMENTATION
SYSTEM

ILS/TACAN

foundation of its air combat efficiency.

When the F-15 was designed its primary mission of air superiority depended on an advanced fire control radar. The daunting specification numbered among its requirements: use in a single-seat aircraft to track targets at extremely long ranges; close-in and look-down operation that would blind other radars; a clutter-free radar display which would show all target information; the ability to provide tracking and steering data on a head up display (HUD) allowing the pilot to keep his eyes on the target; ease of operation; weapons control and coordination; and selected air-to-ground capabilities. In addition it was expected to reach high standards of reliability and maintainability.

Such a requirement would have been unthinkable a few years earlier and showed just how much influence the new electronics could have on the capabilities of a new aircraft. Even so, to meet the specification certain compromises had to be reached and innovative techniques employed to the full.

Most airborne radars work in the X-band (8–12.5GHz) and choice of frequency is the first area of compromise. The critical factor in an aircraft is the size of the antenna: in a fighter the most convenient position is in the nose, where space is restricted by aerodynamic considerations. It so happens that X band produces a good compromise antenna size. Dropping to S band demands a larger antenna, while going further up, say to K band, offers a small and neater antenna but a signal which is adversely affected by meteorological conditions such as rain – hardly a good choice for a modern fighter aircraft.

Pulse repition frequency

Another fundamental choice is that of the pulse repetition frequency (PRF) which refers to the number of transmitted pulses per second. This is often classed as high or low, with high considered to be energy transmitted at 100,000 or more pulses per second while low is only some 1,000 pulses per second. In general terms, the use of a high PRF in the pulse-Doppler radars common in fighters gives good long-range detection of head-on targets, but a restricted detection of tail-on targets and a tendency to lose track of manoeuvring targets.

In comparison, the low-PRF radars then commonly employed for air combat proved to be good for ground mapping but could not detect targets in a look-down mode. It seemed that the compromise choice of a medium PRF would offer improved performance against manoeuvring targets, but at the expense of long range detection.

Hughes overcame the difficulty by developing a radar that had all three PRF modes. High and medium operate together, while low is used for ground mapping. So emerged the APG-63 multi-mode pulse-Doppler radar with an all-altitude, all-aspect attack capability and a maximum detection range in excess of 100 miles (160km). It can also guide radar-controlled missiles against all

CANOPY CONTROL

ENVIRONMENTAL
CONTROL SYSTEM

INTERIOR
LIGHTS

ENGINE
CONTROL
PANEL

NAVIGATION
CONTROL

COMPASS
CONTROL

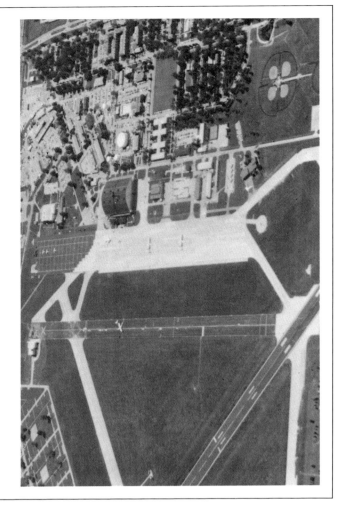

Below: The radar display format used in the Strike Eagle includes a window which can be moved to select enlarged patch maps.

Bottom: Comparative effective ranges of the F-15's APG-63 and the MiG-25's Fox Fire radars, showing the former's clear advantage.

Above: Scott AFB, Illinois, as seen by the camera (right) and as an 8.5ft (2.6m) resolution ground map produced by the F-15 AFCD radar.

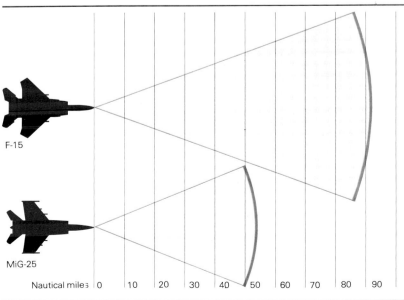

types of target. The primary radar controls are mounted on the aircraft's throttle so allowing the pilot to keep his head up during combat. The HUD shows target positioning, steering, range data and weapons release data.

The radar display provides a clear, clutter-free presentation and look-down view of any target aircraft even in the presence of heavy ground clutter. This ability is the result of a combination of both high and low PRF; digital processing of data, and the use of Kalman filtering in the tracking loops. The last process is a computer technique which continually compares the relative errors of the on-board equipment and data from the external sensors – in other words, a form of averaging of available data. In addition, the radar uses a gridded travelling wave tube that permits variation of the radar waveform to suit the prevailing situation.

Another problem with radar is that of false alarms. These are eliminated by the use of a low-sidelobe antenna – which is a good preventative against enemy EW – a guard receiver and frequency rejection of ground clutter and ground moving targets. Air-to-ground modes include target ranging for automated weapon release, a mapping mode for navigation and, thanks to the Doppler element, a velocity update for the INS. The nose-mounted antenna is a planar array that is hydraulically driven and gimballed in three axes.

Combat evaluation

When the radar first came into operation in the F-15 a series of air combat evaluations were carried out by USAF pilots flying the aircraft against seven different types of aircraft modified to simulate leading threats, and the F-15 won by a handsome margin. More significantly, perhaps, it took part in a series of exercises in which an E-3A Sentry AWACS faces attack by a large force. The F-15 proved to be successful in 38 out of 39 intercepts and its radar overcame the effects of jamming techniques.

Further improvement came with the

development of a programmable signal processor (PSP). This is a feature of all new APG-63s and is available as a retrofit item to earlier models. When it appeared, in 1979, this was the only known deployed PSP and was considered to be a key element in expanding the F-15's tactical air interdiction role while enhancing its tactical air superiority capability. The PSP is a high-speed, special-purpose computer which controls the radar modes through its software rather than through a hard wired circuit design; this allows rapid switching of modes for maximum operational flexibility. PSP-modified radar is fitted to the 420th and subsequent Eagles, which are designated F-15C (single-seat) and F-16D (two-seat).

The use of the PSP paved the way for the modification of an ANAPG-63 to provide synthetic aperture radar (SAR). The modification followed on from earlier SAR work in the USAF Forward-looking Advanced Multimode Radar (FLAMR) programme. The PSP in this instance is a fourth-generation model which performs over seven million operations per second.

SAR imagery sharpens mapping details and provides the pilot with an overhead view, as if he were flying directly over the target, when in fact he can be 100 miles (160km) away. Previously, such imagery had to be processed on the ground because suitable equipment was too large to be easily fitted into an aircraft and processing speed was too slow for real time display.

The first flight of the new radar in an F-15 took place in November 1980, and initially a radar mapping resolution of 127ft (39m) was obtained. Within a month it was down to 60ft (18m) – still not good enough for the recognition of small tactical targets. By the 40th test flight, however, resolution was down to the stipulated level of just 10ft (3m).

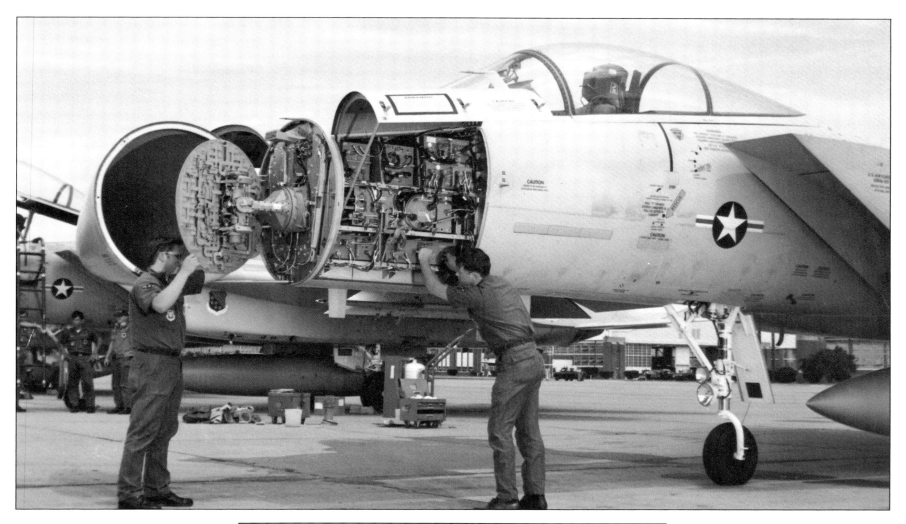

This degree of resolution means that at a distance of 20–30 miles (30–50km) from the target street patterns, power lines and field boundaries are visible. At 10 miles (16km) from an airfield a ⅔-mile (1km) square radar map can be displayed and aircraft as little as 8ft 6in (2.6m) apart can be clearly recognized. Other targets may be seen equally clearly, making target selection easy and unambiguous. The radar maps are updated every few seconds and linked to the navigation systems and weapons modes for ground attack preparations.

By this time, too, MCAIR had developed low-drag fuel pallets to increase the F-15's ferry range. These are two close fitting packs known as fuel and sensor tactical (FAST) packs. In addition to increased fuel tankage, the FAST packs allow a greater range of electronic sensors to be carried, including optical cameras, low light level TV cameras and a laser designator.

Enhanced Eagles

Coincident with this development, the manufacturers suggested that the USAF needed an all-weather fighter capable of performing long-range, air-to-ground interdiction missions while maintaining its air-to-air capabilities, and suggested than an enhanced Eagle would fulfil these requirements.

Two-seater F-15 Eagles had been built and were externally identifiable only by their larger cockpit canopy. This allowed them to function as trainers as well as being combat capable. The manufacturer used one of these two-seaters in a company-funded project known as Strike Eagle to create an all-weather, day/night ground attack aircraft using the new SAR radar integrated with forward looking infra-red (FLIR) system of the Pave Tack pod. The rear cockpit was modified to allow a specialist crew member to handle the radar and FLIR inputs.

The rear cockpit was fitted with four electronic displays and two hand controllers which allow the crew member to focus his attention on the displays while operating systems and controlling

1 Antenna
2 Analog processor
3 Power supply
4 Data processor
5 Digital processor
6 Transmitter
7 Exciter
8 Receiver

1 Antenna
2 Power supply
3 Data processor
4 Signal processor
5 Transmitter
6 Analog signal converter
7 Receiver/exciter

Above: Comparison of the standard APG-63 (top) and the PSP-modified equipment carried by the F-15C.

display content. Two of the displays are used for navigational purposes, one for weapon selection and one to monitor enemy tracking systems.

At the same time, improving electronic systems had created more sensitive electronic countermeasures sensors and the manufacturers proposed an Advanced Wild Weasel F-15. The outcome of these projects is described elsewhere in this book though they deserve mention in the evolution of the aircraft's avionic systems.

In 1981, another advanced avionic feature became linked with the F-15,

when the Integrated Flight/Fire Control (IFFC) and Firefly III programmes were initiated. The IFFC 1 programme, being undertaken by MCAIR under a \$14 million contract from the Air Force Flight Dynamics Laboratory, is for the design, development, integration and flight testing of a system which couples the Eagle's fire control and flight control systems to accept dual control inputs and tailor flight control response to the various weapons delivery modes. The Firefly III programme, being conducted by the General Electric Aircraft Equipment Division under a \$7 million Air Force Avionics Laboratory contract for the further development of the fire control system.

The IFFC/Firefly III coupling will

Above: Routine maintenance on an F-15A's APG-63 radar. All the equipment is readily accessible, and individual components are easily removable for repair.

allow automatic positioning of the aircraft to attack targets detected by an electro-optical target designation pod. This is expected to shorten engagement times and enable the aircraft to drop its bombs or stores without having to overfly the target. The F-15 in the Firefly programme carries a Martin Marietta-built Atlis II designator pod in the port forward missile well and this is linked to the aircraft's fly-by-wire system via an intermediate additional digital computer.

As had been predicted by the manufacturers at the start of the Strike Eagle project, the USAF is becoming acutely aware of its need to have a long-range all-weather aircraft with a good air-to-ground capability. The current F-4 is nearing retirement and the possibility of an all-new multi-role fighter is unlikely to be translated into reality much before the mid-1990s.

A more practical solution would seem to be the upgrading and modification of an existing aircraft, principally through the use of improved avionics. This is now the subject of a USAF programme which is comparing the relative performances of the F-15 and F-16. Three F-15 advanced fighter demonstrators will be used to evaluate both single pilot and pilot/specialist officer crew complements. The single-seater is an F-15C; one two-seat F-15D is fitted with a Ford Aerospace FLIR and laser tracker/marker pod while the other two-seater is the original Strike Eagle with Pave Tack FLIR and laser pod and synthetic aperture radar. The rear cockpit of the last is still configured with an array of special displays and controls for operation of the sensors, and the aircraft is now known as the Advanced Fighter Capability Demonstrator. Although the Pave Tack pod is expected to be the standard fit, it was considered prudent to gain additional operational experience by using the Ford Aerospace system, which has been derived from a similar pod developed for the F/A-18 Hornet.

Another alternative option for the enhanced Eagle is the Martin Marietta LANTIRN (Low Altitude Navigation and Targeting Infra-Red for Night) system currently under development for the USAF's F-16 and A-10 aircraft. The system consists of two pods and cockpit displays: the navigation pod contains a wide-field-of-view FLIR sensor, terrain-following radar and associated electronics, while the targeting pod contains a stabilized wide- and narrow-field-of-view targeting FLIR sensor, automatic trackers, laser designator and ranger, automatic target recognizer, missile boresight correlator and supporting electronics. Interface with the pilot is through a wide-field-of-view, diffractive optics HUD, built by Marconi Avionics in the UK. The system is still under development, and its inclusion on an enhanced Eagle is subject to its successful service entry on the F-16 and A-10.

Possibly the greatest operational

Below: Modifications introduced on the IFFC/Firefly III flight and fire control system, compared with the standard F-15 system.

problem that has to be overcome in the advanced role is that of survivability. This can be achieved only by the use of advanced sensors and more capable avionics, probably with a two-man crew, while Visionics will be needed for all-weather, low-altitude flight using terrain-following radar and a new radar altimeter. Some of this innovation will evolve as part of the constant product improvement programme that companies tend to pursue during the lifetime of their products. In the USAF this is epitomized by the Multi-Stage Improvement Programme (MSIP) which is currently monitoring enhanced radar, improved software and the introduction

of Seek Talk and JTIDS.

Seek Talk is the codename for a long term programme to reduce the vulnerability of UHF radios to enemy jamming by modifying existing radios with the addition of spread spectrum techniques and the use of a null steering antenna.

JTIDS stands for Joint Tactical Information Distribution System, an ambitious programme intended to provide a high-capacity, reliable, jam-resistant, secure, digital information distribution system which will allow for a very high degree of interoperability between various elements of deployed forces and command and control centres. An interesting feature of the JTIDS system is a

relevant navigation characteristic: Implicit in the signalling structure is a highly accurate measurement of message time of arrival which is readily convertible to transmitter/receiver range. This could prove to be a most useful device in future tactical roles and in a supplementary role to INS, whose principal virtue is its independence of ground installations.

Although a great deal of current development is obscured by the needs of security it is possible to visualise an advanced version of the F-15 in the required role. Current systems of the Strike Eagle standard could be integrated with the results of the Firefly III programme and with new HUDs such as the Marconi Avionics wide field-of-view diffractive-optics system. These systems would operate in conjunction with advanced versions of missiles, guns and laser-guided bombs. Trials were due to start in 1983 of the AGM-65D IIR Maverick air-to-ground missile and the General Electric 30mm gun pod.

The next event in the evolving avionic scene will be the introduction of the Global Positioning System (GPS), which

Left: The IFFC/Firefly III F-15B, with Martin Marietta ATLIS II optical sensor and tracker pod on the port wing missile pylon.

Below: Typical manoeuvring attack made possible by the IFFC system (bottom) compared with the conventional pop-up attack profile.

is expected to revolutionize navigation, though it requires satellites which could be vulnerable in war. Currently two F-15s are conducting GPS trials and it is expected that the complete system will be operational by 1987. It will eventually consist of a network of Navstar satellites circling the earth. Thousands of ground receivers mounted in all types of military vehicles and even carried by foot soldiers will translate satellite signals into navigation information that will be accurate to within 10–20m anywhere in the world, day or night and regardless of weather. The information will include altitude, longitude, latitude, velocity to 0.1m/sec and a precise time in nanoseconds.

The Navstar satellites will orbit the earth at an altitude of 12,500 miles (20,000km), each one continuously broadcasting time and position messages. This information will greatly enhance tactical air operations and should prove to be a potent all-weather navigation system. Advanced anti-jamming techniques are built into the system to permit continuing operation under the most stringent of enemy EW operations.

The GPS tactical air configuration will provide continuous signal tracking under all flight conditions and the system will be integrated with other on-board avionics so that the GPS-derived data can be used to refine other flight systems.

Below: Illuminated indicators on the front panel include fire warning (top left), canopy unlocked (top right), air-to-ground mode button and beacon light (centre) landing gear (bottom left) and caution panel (bottom right).

Armament

The missiles-only fighters produced for the USAF in the late 1950s and early 1960s were found to be at a severe disadvantage over Vietnam, and the Eagle weapon system was planned from the outset to include a gun. At the same time, improved versions of the medium-range, radar-guided Sparrow and short-range, heat-seeking Sidewinder were provided. New weapons planned for the Eagle include the AIM-120 AMRAAM, while the type has also proved able to deliver air-to-ground weapons with a high degree of accuracy, leading to the possibility of orders for a dual-role fighter development.

The basic requirements of the Eagle weapons system, as outlined in the Development Concept fall into three distinct categories: guns, air-to-air missiles and air-to-ground weaponry. In addition, we must also consider the use of external fuel and EW pods to enhance the basic capability of the Eagle.

During the late 1950s and early 1960s air combat with guns was thought by many to have had its day, and the latest American fighters had no guns, relying solely on air-to-air missiles. Air combat during the Vietnam War, however, revealed such an urgent need for gun armament that a new version of the F-4

Phantom, TAC's principal fighter, had to be developed with an internal 20mm gun.

From the beginning, therefore, the FX was planned with an internal gun as an integral part of its weapons system. Initial production models were to rely on the tried and true M61A1 20mm Vulcan cannon, produced by the Aircraft Equipment Division of the General Electric Company. Later models of the Eagle were to have a new 25mm cannon, using a new type of caseless ammunition, which would have the advantage of eliminating cartridge extraction and ejection systems, resulting in a

simpler mechanism. General Electric and Philco-Ford (now Ford Aerospace and Communications) both submitted designs, and after evaluation in December 1971 Philco-Ford was awarded the contract for the new gun, designated the GAU-7.

Although potentially a simpler weapon, the advantages mentioned above were offset by other problems, basically involving the ammunition. With caseless ammunition there is no spent cartridge to be wasted (or collected) after the round is fired, promising potentially enormous savings. However, the US Army had been trying to get caseless ammunition right for the previous 15 years with a continuing lack of success. (The world's first weapon designed with a successful caseless ammunition is the Heckler & Koch G-11 rifle, with ammunition from H&K in collaboration with Dynamit Nobel.)

The GAU-7 ammunition was being developed by the Brunswick Corporation. The propellant half of the 25mm round was covered with a flame retardant covering, which was stripped off mechanically as the rounds entered a

conveyor which took them to the five barrels of the weapon. This stripping mechanism was causing the ammunition conveyor to jam. Another problem involved the development of a moisture-protective material for use with the ammunition, whose final drawback was inconsistent ballistic action. In theory the higher muzzle velocity of 4,000ft/sec (1,200m/sec), compared with the 3,200ft/sec (975m/sec) of the M61, meant that not only did the projectile reach the target sooner than an M61 round, but also that it had a flatter trajectory, producing a more concentrated hit pattern on the target and giving a higher probability of kill. Unfortunately, the whole system proved too unreliable.

By September 1973, with over $100 million spent on development, the problems with the GAU-7 had still to be overcome, and with other new-technology items on the Eagle running reasonably smoothly, the Air Force decided to

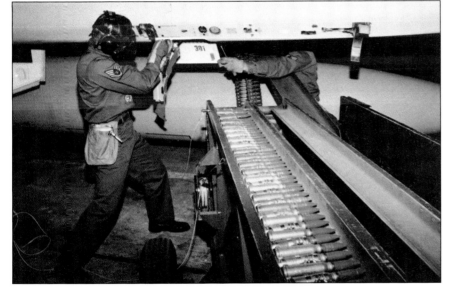

Above: F-15 in standard air superiority configuration, with four AIM-7s and four AIM-9s.

Left: Armourers use a conveyor belt to load 20mm ammunition into an F-15 ammunition drum. The links are stripped during the loading process.

Below: Radar-guided Sparrow for BVR engagements and short-range Sidewinders form a potent combination.

Right: Missile launch as seen from the back of a two-seat F-15. At one stage the USAF switched to an all-missile armament, but during the Vietnam war the F-4 had to be revised to accommodate a gun, since many engagements took place at ranges too short for a missile to be launched effectively.

Left: The General Electric M61 Vulcan 20mm gun system, and details of its location in the F-15 airframe. The gun could not be mounted in the nose, since this would interfere with the radar, and the wing root alternative was found to be eminently satisfactory. The ammunition drum, housing 940 rounds, is mounted in the centre fuselage; a linkless feed system transports the rounds to the gun and carries the spent cartridge cases back again. This system has proved extremely reliable in operation.

cut its losses. Although Philco-Ford proposed a year's delay on the programme, it was cancelled and replaced by the M61, of 1954 vintage.

The M61A1 is an exceptionally reliable system. Its rotary action allows a rate of fire of some 6,000 rounds per minute (although only 940 rounds are carried on the Eagle). The use of six barrels minimizes erosion, thus ensuring long life for the weapon. The high rates of fire dictate a special linkless feed for the M61, and while some aircraft systems expel the used cases, others collect them. The ammunition used is in the M50 series, and includes armour piercing (with or without tracer elements) and incendiary types. The rotary action of the weapon as installed in the F-15 is provided by hydraulic/electrical power.

Locating the gun

The choice of location for the internal gun was not easy. Ideally it should have been placed as close to the fighter's cg as possible in order to reduce aiming errors when the weapon was fired, but a nose mounting was ruled out because the vibration of the weapon firing would upset the microcircuitry of the APG-63 radar. A second location, further aft on the fuselage centreline, was rejected because of possible gun-gas ingestion problems. The final solution, approached with some trepidation was to mount the gun in the starboard wing root, where there was plenty of room for the weapon and its ammunition drum and feed system. Tests later showed that the comparitively large separation of the gun from the fore-and-aft axis of the aircraft produced no aiming or recoil problems. In addition, the gun alignment could more easily be varied to give maximum tracking time on target, a facility initially demonstrated in simulation, and later proved in practice.

For the future, there is a new General Electric 25mm cannon, the GAU-12/U, under development for the AV-8B Harrier II/Harrier GR.5. Present plans do not call for its use beyond the AV-8B, but the possibility exists that it might be adapted for installation in the F-15E. Another gun option for the F-15E is the carriage of three General Electric GE 430 GEPOD-30 30mm gun pods on fuselage and underwing pylons. The GEPOD-30 is a lightweight four-barrel version of the GAU-8/A gun used in the A-10A Thunderbolt II, and fires the standard GAU-8/A ammunition. The main role of the GEPOD-30 would be

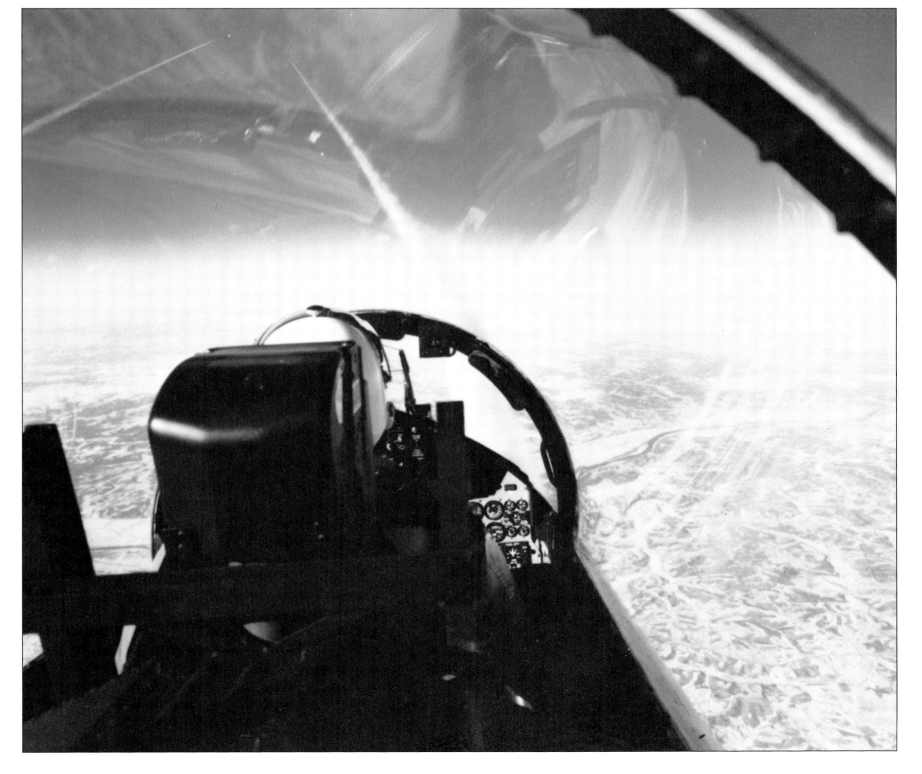

air-to-ground, but there is nothing to preclude its use in the air-to-air mode if the tactical situation allows.

Although the gun has been restored, the missile remains the Eagle's primary air-to-air weapon. The new fighter's missile armament was originally to consist of the AIM-7F Sparrow for beyond visual range (BVR) engagements, and a new short-range IR-homing missile, designated AIM-82. The latter missile was cancelled well before it reached the hardware stage, and the AIM-9L Sidewinder took over. For the future, the AIM-120 AMRAAM will replace Sparrow, with the projected European ASRAAM a possible successor to Sidewinder.

AIM-7 Sparrow

The AIM-7 Sparrow originated as Sperry Gyroscope's Project Hot Shot in 1946, and by 1955 it was in service as the beam-riding AAM-N-2 Sparrow I with the US Navy. The active-radar Sparrow II was cancelled in 1957 and the AIM-7F comes from the third generation of Sparrow, the Raytheon AAM-N-6 Sparrow III, which became the AIM-7C when the US services changed nomenclature in 1962. The AIM-7C introduced semi-active radar homing with continuous wave (CW) guidance and was in service by 1958. The AIM-7E, later versions of which armed early Eagles, featured a continuous-rod warhead, consisting of a 66lb (30kg) explosive charge enclosed in a tight drum made from a continuous rod of stainless steel. On detonation, this rod shatters into some 2,500 lethal fragments. The more manoeuvrable AIM-7E2 was developed to reduce the missile's minimum range as a result of experience in Vietnam, when the demand for visual identification of targets inhibited its use, and this version armed the initial batches of F-15 Eagles.

The AIM-7F, designated missile for the Eagle, brought the Sparrow into the solid-state electronic age. Reducing the size and weight of the guidance package, still CW, allowed a more powerful motor, the Hercules Mk 58, to be used, resulting in an increased range of 62 miles (100km), and enabling a larger 88lb (40kg) warhead to be carried. Introduced in 1977, the AIM-7F is claimed to be able to lock-on to a target against clutter up to 10dB.

The most recent version of the Sparrow is the AIM-7M, which has an inverse monopulse seeker, a digital signal processor, a new autopilot and a new fuze. It is expected to offer greatly

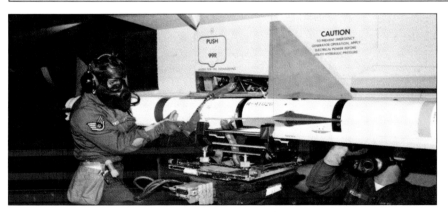

Above: The Sparrow accelerates towards its maximum speed of approximately Mach 4. Range of the AIM-7F is 62 miles (100km).

Left: Armourers in protective clothing and respirators install a Sparrow on its fuselage mounting.

Below: In its air superiority configuration, the F-15 can have its fuel, oil and liquid oxygen replenished, and Sparrows and ammunition reloaded, in a turnaround time of only 12 minutes.

improved results in adverse weather conditions, as well as in an ECCM environment, and starting with the FY 1981 budget funding, Sparrow production has been concentrated on this variant.

AIM-9 Sidewinder

The Sidewinder is the original simple, low-cost air-to-air missile, capable of being carried by practicaly any combat aircraft. Since its development in 1949 by a team of scientists at the Naval Ordnance Test Station (now the Naval Weapons Centre) at China Lake, it has been produced in seven major variants, with at least one further derivative under consideration. US production of the initial AIM-9B variant reached a total of 80,900 missiles, while a European consortium produced about 15,000. The usefulness of the missile is exemplified by the fact that during the Falklands conflict of 1982 the RAF modified their Nimrod maritime patrol and ASW aircraft to carry four Sidewinders in a matter of weeks in order to give them a measure of self-defence capability.

Sidwinder has an infra-red seeker which homes onto heat emissions from the jet efflux of the target. A variety of guidance heads, and six major forward fin configurations have been used, and many of the later versions combined older airframes with new seekers and fins. The AIM-9L, which represents the third generation of the missile, features a new double-delta forward fin configuration of larger span than previous missiles and a new seeker head. Part of the DSQ-29 guidance and control system, the new head uses AM-FM conical scan, with a fixed-reticle, tilted-mirror system, and is cooled by Argon gas. The new seeker offers greater sensitivity and improved tracking stability, while lethality is increased by the use of the DSU-15B active optical laser fuze, allied to the WDU-17B annular blast fragmentation warhead.

Once the pilot has energized the missile homing head, he listens for the 'growl' in his headset that signifies it has acquired a target. Should he be set up for a perfect shot straight up the tailpipe of a target, the growl intensifies to a strident tone, and the pilot launches the missile. In this respect Sidewinders (of whatever mark) are simple to use in air-to-air combat.

AIM-120 AMRAAM

Despite all the advances made over the years with the Sparrow AAM, it retains one basic drawback – its semi-active radar guidance system requires the target to be continuously illuminated throughout an engagement, so that the pilot can only deal with one target at a time. Consequently, the prime require-

ment during development of the Advanced Medium Range Air-to-Air Missile (AMRAAM) was that it should be a launch-and-leave missile, allowing several targets to be engaged simultaneously beyond visual range without monopolizing the fire-control radar and leaving the pilot blind to other threats. AMRAAM was also required to be

usable in all weathers, fired from or at all aspects and with a look-down/shoot-down capability. With the proliferation of Sparrow throughout the US Air Force, Navy and Marine Corps, it had to be able to integrate with existing fighters and fire control radar, and physically fit where a Sparrow was previously located. The final requirement was con-

siderably higher reliability than that of Sparrow.

This was a demanding specification, and in 1976 a joint USAF/US Navy project office was set up at Elgin AFB to organize the development of the new missile. By February 1979 the conceptual studies had been narrowed down to submissions from Hughes Aircraft and Raytheon, who were awarded contracts for ten prototype missiles each to be fired from F-14, F-15 and F-16 aircraft in a competitive evaluation.

After only three firings of each contender the trials were halted, with the Hughes entry a clear winner, and in December 1981 the company received a 50-month full scale development contract valued at some $421 million. The resulting missile, designated AIM-120 but still known as AMRAAM at the time of writing, is some two-thirds of the weight of the Sparrow, and similar in configuration, though the main fins are somewhat smaller. It has an estimated speed of Mach 4, and an active X-band radar terminal seeker using a high-power solid-state transmitter with a low-sidelobe, wide-gimbal antenna, and a built-in radio-frequency processor. Navigation, autopilot, radar, datalink, fuzing, sequencing and self-test functions are all handled by a single 30MKz microprocessor.

The last two of the Hughes test firings were from an F-15, following one from an F-16, and the second launch, on November 23, 1981, scored a direct hit on a QF-102 target drone. The F-15 was flying at 6,000ft (1,830m) at Mach 0.75, and the missile was launched in a look-down/shoot-down mode at the QF-102 flying at 1,000ft (300m) at Mach 0.7. The missile was cued by the APG-63 radar and launched by the aircraft's stores

Top left: A fully armed F-15 stands ready for takeoff, with safety tags on missiles and airframe and cockpit canopy open.

Centre left: An armourer removes the cover from the seeker head of a Sidewinder as the aircraft is prepared for a sortie.

Left: Mock-up of the Hughes AIM-120 AMRAAM is assembled on the fuselage station of an F-15.

Below left: First captive flight test of a Hughes AMRAAM Instrumented Measurement Vehicle, used to test the new missile's aerodynamic compatibility with the F-15.

Below: During the firing trials that resulted in its selection, a prototype of the Hughes AMRAAM is launched from an F-15B.

control system. It demonstrated inertial midcourse guidance and then acquired its target against ground clutter.

The final prototype firing came late in 1982 and demonstrated the missile's ability to intercept a low-flying aircraft using self-screening ECM. It was launched from an F-15 flying at 16,000ft (4,900m) some 10.8nm from a QF-102 drone flying towards the launch aircraft at 400ft (120m). It was launched with command-inertial guidance and then switched to active radar in order to acquire and intercept the target, which passed within lethal range of the AMRAAM's warhead.

Further development firings are scheduled to take place in 1984 from the F-16 (on which the AIM-120 will enter service in 1986) followed by the F-18, F-15 and F-14. The USAF requirement

for AIM-120 is upwards of 20,000 missiles, and already further improvements are planned for the missile's 25-year projected life. The AIM-120B will feature passive terminal homing, and will be introduced from 1990, while the AIM-120C will have overall improvements in range, speed and manoeuvreability, and will be available from the mid-1990s. All variants of the AIM-120 will be able to be launched from either rails or ejection units.

AMRAAM is the subject of an agreement signed between the United States and France, Germany and the UK, which will see the missile become the NATO-standard BVR weapon. In turn, the European partners will develop the Advanced Short Range Air-to-Air Missile (ASRAAM) to replace Sidewinder in both US and European service. Al-

though agreements over ASRAAM are in existence, the missile is unlikely to be available before the late 1980s.

Air-to-ground Weapons
While primarily an air superiority fighter, the Eagle possesses a substantial air-to-ground secondary capability, as the accompanying table illustrates. Work is also under way on a dedicated air-to-ground variant, designated F-15E, which will be a two-seat strike fighter. The basic stores capability of the F-15A/C has five weapons pylons, in addition to the four Sparrow missiles, capable of carrying up to 16,000lb (7,257kg) of bombs, rockets, ECM equipment or external fuel tanks.

The Strike Eagle demonstrator, on which the F-15E will be based, can carry up to 24,000lb (10,886kg) of stores. Among the stores compatible with the Eagle in this role are the AGM-88A High-speed Anti-Radiation Missile (HARM), AGM-65 Maverick TV-guided missile, AGM-84A Harpoon anti-ship missile, Mk 20 Rockeye bombs on MER-200 multiple ejection racks, Matra Durandal runway denial weapons, 500lb (227kg) Mk 82 bombs in Slick (low-drag) and Snakeye (retarded) configuration, 2,000lb (907kg) Mk 84 bombs in Slick, Laser, Electro-optical and Infrared homing versions, ALQ-131 ECM pods and 600US gal (500Imp gal/2,280 litre) drop tanks.

1 ECM antenna
2 ALQ-119(V) jammer pod
3 600US gal (500Imp gal/2,273 litre) fuel tank
4 MER (multiple ejector rack) carrying three Mk 82 500lb (227kg) slick (low-drag) general-purpose bombs (one with a stand-off contact fuze) plus one AIM-9J and one AIM-9L Sidewinder AAMs
5 FAST (Fuel and sensor tactical) pack conformal fuel tank
6 MK 20 Rockeye cluster bomb
7 Tactical nuclear bomb
8 MK 82 Snakeye high-drag bomb
9 M61 cannon with 940 rounds of 20mm ammunition
10 GBU-10E/B (Mk 84 2,000lb) Paveway II laser-guided bomb
11 AVQ-26 Pave Tack sensor pod

12 GBU-12D/B (Mk 82 500lb) Paveway II laser-guided bomb
13 CBU-52B/B cluster bomb dispenser
14 AIM-7F/M Sparrow AAM
15 AGM-84A Harpoon anti-ship missile
16 SUU-20 practice bomb dispenser
17 MK 84 2,000lb (907kg) general-purpose bomb
18 GBU-15(V)-4-B modular guided glide bomb
19 AGM-88A Harm anti-radar missile
20 AGM-65D IIR (imaging infra-red) Maverick air-to-surface missile
21 Two AGM-65A (TV) or AGM-65C (laser) Mavericks
22 General Electric GPU-5/A gun pod housing 30mm GAU-13/A gun, ammunition and drive system
23 AIM-120 AMRAAM (advanced medium-range air-to-air missile)

The MER-200 multiple ejection bomb rack is designated BRU-26A/A, and allows the Eagle a high degree of flexibility in its weapons carriage. It is in production to equip all Eagles assigned to the US Rapid Deployment Joint Task Force, as well as for the Japanese Air Self Defense Force F-15Js. Its main advantage is that it allows supersonic carriage and release of up to six weapons, and can jettison them in any loading configuration. It is strong enough to allow the pilot to pull 7.3g during combat manoeuvres, and has been flight tested to Mach 1.4, although MCAIR, the manufacturers, claim carriage, jettison and release of stores up to Mach 2. Production of this low drag multiple ejection rack was running at 40 units per month by mid-1983.

In addition, the Eagle can enhance its range by the use of the FAST (Fuel And Sensor Tactical) packs mounted on the fuselage side, and these retain the ability to mount Sparrow or AMRAAM missiles on the lower corners, or carry some 4,400lb (1,996kg) of air-to-ground stores. Each of the FAST packs can carry 849US gal (707Imp gal/3,228 litres) of fuel. Alternatively, or in combination with fuel, they can house cameras and IR sensors for reconnaissance; low-light television (LLTV), forward looking IR (FLIR) and laser designators for the strike role; or Wild Weasel equipment for defence suppression.

FAST packs were first flown on an F-15B on July 27, 1974. MCAIR claim that carriage of the conformal tanks only slightly reduces the subsonic profile drag relative to the clean aircraft and represent only a fraction of the super-

sonic drag of the three standard drop tanks, which between them carry 20 per cent more fuel than the FAST packs. Installation or removal is possible in 15 minutes, despite their complex shape Pand size. With FAST packs and the three drop tanks, the F-15C has demonstrated an unrefuelled ferry range of 2,660nm (4,903km). In this configuration, the F-15C has a maximum gross weight of 68,000lb (30,840kg), while the F-15D model is only some 800lb (363kg) heavier with the same internal fuel.

Weapons configurations
In the basic air-to-air role, the F-15A/C Eagle carries four AIM-7F Sparrows, four AIM-9L Sidewinders and the internal 20mm gun. In addition, it usually carries a 600US gal drop tank on the centre-line pylon, and the inner wing

pylon can also carry a similar drop tank without sacrificing the Sidewinder capability.

The basic attack configuration of the non-dedicated Eagle retains the basic air-to-air configuration, possibly including the centre-line tank, and adds extra stores. Any range enhancements required can be provided by air-to-air refuelling. The prime requirement was for the attack mission not to detract from the basic air-to-air combat mission, which is certainly the case.

Below: The second F-15B in early 1976, before its development into the Strike Eagle. Even at this stage MCAIR were keen to demonstrate the F-15's ground-attack capability, and 71-0291 is seen here armed with 18 500lb (227kg) Mk 82 slicks.

Left: The impressive array of stores that have been launched by the Eagle or are designed to be compatible with the aircraft's delivery system.

23

22

19

18

17

16

5

Right: Multiple stores can be carried by a standard F-15 without disrupting the normal armament of Sparrows and Sidewinders.

Deployment and Combat

Following its service introduction with the 'Triple Nickel' 555th TFTS, the Eagle achieved operational status in 1976 with the 1st Tactical Fighter Wing. Subsequently the type has been deployed with USAF units in Europe, the Far East and Alaska, as well as equipping selected units of TAC's Air Defense Command, while export customers have included Israel, Japan and Saudi Arabia. Only Israeli pilots have seen combat in the type, achieving predictably impressive results: elsewhere, the F-15 continues to be the USAF's principal front-line fighter.

The operational career of the F-15 effectively began on November 14, 1974, at Luke AFB, Arizona, when President Gerald Ford accepted TF-15A 73-0108 on behalf of Tactical Air Command (TAC). The Eagle had been flying in full USAF insignia for some time by then, but the handful of Air Force units which had used the type prior to November 1974 were essentially test organizations, unlike the 58th Tactical Fighter Training Wing (TFTW), the unit which was to operate the first TF-15A. This aircraft, incidentally, was christened 'TAC 1' during the ceremonies that marked the type's introduction to service.

The first F-15 squadron was the 555th Tactical Fighter Training Squadron

Below: Ready to get airborne on an interception in less than five minutes, a fully-armed F-15A waits in its hardened shelter.

(TFTS). This unit, the famed 'Triple Nickel', had racked up an impressive air combat record in Vietnam when, equipped with another MCAIR product, the F-4 Phantom. It accounted for no less than 40 MiGs. The 555th quickly set about the task of qualifying instructor pilots and formulating a training syllabus, a process which was largely completed by about the middle of 1975 when personnel earmarked to serve with the first fully operational wing were present in some considerable numbers at Luke.

Mission-ready status

The responsibility of bringing TAC's newest piece of hardware to mission-ready status was entrusted to the 1st Tactical Fighter Wing (TFW), which shared Langley AFB, Virginia, with TAC headquarters, and the next 18 months or so proved to be a period of

intense activity at this base as more and more personnel were posted in to join the team.

As with most modern combat aircraft, introduction of the Eagle did not go entirely according to plan. One of the most significant difficulties concerned delays in the output of qualified pilots by the 58th TFTW, this arising directly from the rather lower than anticipated sortie production rate (SPR). In fact, low SPR levels affected the entire project for quite some time, and although the decision in November 1975 to eliminate the air-to-ground portion of the training syllabus went some way towards alleviating the pilot shortage, the situation was compounded by the AIMVAL/ACEVAL (Air Intercept Missile Evaluation/Air Combat Evaluation) test programme of 1976-77 which called for the 58th TFTW to surrender six aircraft to the 57th Fighter Weapons Wing (FWW) at

Above: An unarmed 36th TFW F-15A on deployment over Norway. The 36th was the first USAFE unit to be equipped with the Eagle.

Nellis. An example of the effect that these difficulties had on the overall pace of the project is provided by the fact that the 1st TFW was still some 18 pilots short of its authorized level in May 1976, about five months after it had been fully equipped with 72 Eagles.

A key factor in the SPR shortfall was the low rate of aircraft serviceability during the early stages of the Eagle's career mainly because of difficulties involving the F100 engine and the fire control system and its associated APG-63 radar. Engine-related problems such as compressor stalls, slow acceleration and stagnation with a corresponding loss of thrust have continued to cause concern and were certainly not helped by the production difficulties experienced by Pratt & Whitney in the late 1970s.

As far as the avionics are concerned, the picture is somewhat brighter. Most early problems resulted from poor performance of on-base Avionics Intermediate Shop (AIS) test equipment and the consequent need to send many defective LRUs (Line Replaceable Units) back to the contractor for repair and rectification work. This, in turn, brought about a 'domino' effect as cannibalization became necessary to maintain aircraft in an 'up' condition, the situation eventually reaching a point where, when engine difficulties were taken into account, the expected degree of reliability was being missed by in excess of 50 per cent. Hardware and software fixes incorporated in the latter half of the 1970s have gone some way toward improving avionics performance but AIS test equipment is still causing more than a few headaches for maintenance personnel.

Despite these trials and tribulations, training of 1st TFW personnel forged ahead steadily, being highlighted by delivery of the first F-15A (74-0083 'Peninsula Patriot') to the 27th TFS at Langley on January 9, 1976. By the end of that year two further squadrons, the 71st and 94th TFSs, had also received their allotted number of aircraft and the 1st TFW was fully equipped if not yet fully operational.

Not surprisingly, the pilots spent most of 1976 familiarizing themselves with their new mounts and exploring the capabilities of the F-15 in the air combat role. This involved extensive training exercises against each other and against dissimilar types such as the T-38 Talon, A-4 Skyhawk, F-4 Phantom, F-5E Tiger II and F-106 Delta Dart. The opportunity to participate in Red Flag exercises at Nellis was also taken: during September and October no less than 24 aircraft deployed to Nevada for Red Flag VIII. They performed credit-

ably, the SPR rising significantly along with pilot confidence in the aircraft and its systems.

By the end of 1976 both the 27th TFS and the 71st TFS were adjudged to be mission-ready but the emphasis was already shifting toward Europe, home of the next wing to convert. This was the 36th TFW, then operating the F-4E Phantom from Bitburg AB, West Germany. However, rather than accomplish transition at Bitburg it was decided that a new concept would be used in an attempt to curtail the 'down-time' which is usually associated with major re-equipment programmes. Accordingly, the 1st TFW was tasked with assisting the 36th TFW to attain operational readiness on the F-15 under the code name Ready Eagle.

36th TFW build-up
Maintenance personnel for the 36th TFW duly began training at Langley in September 1976 while aircrew for the first squadron – a mix of experienced F-15 pilots from Luke and Langley plus some former F-4E pilots from Bitburg – gradually accumulated at Langley. Responsibility for overseeing the Langley-based phase of flying training rested with the 94th TFS and was highlighted by the first pilot achieving mission-ready status in mid-January of 1977. On January 5, the first two Eagles had reached Bitburg for maintenance

Above: A trio of F-15As from the famous 555th 'Triple Nickel' TFTS, 58th TFTW, based at Luke AFB, Arizona.

familiarization training, where they were joined by two more during March.

In the meantime, delivery of those Eagles earmarked for service with the 36th TFW was being effected to Langley and it was from here that some 20 F-15As and a trio of TF-15As left for the first mass transatlantic migration to Bitburg on April 27, these all reaching Germany safely during the afternoon of the same day. Within 12 hours of arrival the 525th TFS was in business, some of the new arrivals already standing 'Zulu'

Below: A pair of F-15As from the 1st Tactical Fighter Wing, the first operational Eagle unit, based at TAC's Langley HQ.

Below: A 1st TFW F-15A banks over one of the world's most expensive flight lines at Langley AFB, Virginia, also home of the 48th FIS.

Bottom: Three F-15As and a two-seat F-15B of the 57th Fighter Weapons Wing, based at Nellis AFB, Arizona, in formation.

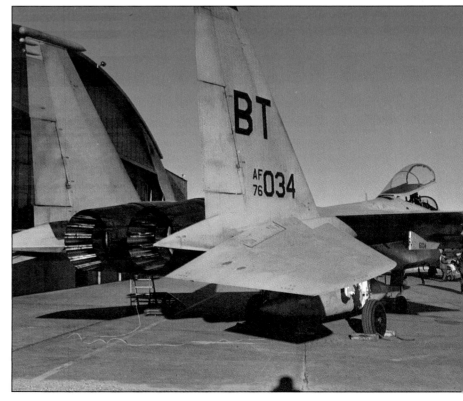

Above: A trio of 36th TFW F-15As during the Arctic Express exercise held in 1978 to test combat readiness in Arctic conditions.

Right: One of the 36th TFW's Bitburg-based F-15As parked outside its hardened aircraft shelter for routine maintenance.

alert duty and providing a fitting testimonial to the success of the initial phase of Ready Eagle.

Back in the USA, training of the second 36th TFW squadron, the 53rd TFS, followed similar lines. Deployment of the 53rd to Bitburg followed in July, while the third squadron – the 22nd TFS – brought the re-equipment process to a successful conclusion when it took up residence at Bitburg in October. It should be noted that transatlantic ferry flights of aircraft for these two squadrons were made over a fairly lengthy period, groups of half-a-dozen or so being deployed at a time during the summer and autumn of 1977 until the planned level of about 80, including several spares was achieved.

Holloman AFB in New Mexico was the next base to welcome the Eagle, re-equipment of the resident 49th TFW's three squadrons being accomplished during 1977-78. Another new procedure, code-named Ready Team, was

employed on this occasion, the intention being to permit some existing fighters – in this case F-4D Phantoms – to remain combat-ready during the initial phases of conversion. The process of transition got under way in June 1977 when the first pilots for the 7th TFS reported to Luke for training with the 58th Tactical Training Wing (TTW) as it had become known during 1977. The 58th TTW had itself been expanded in June 1976 when the 461st TFTS was organized as the second F-15 training squadron, and it grew still further while the 49th TFW was undergoing conversion, gaining the 550th TFTS in September 1977. Initial qualification of the 7th TFS was managed by the 461st and 555th TFTSs, and was followed by a brief assignment to the 550th TFTS for mission-ready checkout, culminating in reassignment to Holloman where F-15s began to arrive in October 1977. Re-equipment of the 8th TFS was accomplished with effect from January 1978 while the 9th

USAF F-15 operating units

Formation	Base	Squadrons	Remarks
1st TFW, TAC	Langley AFB, Virginia	27th TFS 71st TFS 94th TFS	F-15A/B from Jan 76 Re-equipped with F-15C/D from Dec 81
18th TFW, PACAF	Kadena AB, Okinawa	12th TFS 44th TFS 67th TFS	Equipped with F-15C/D 1979–80
1st TFW	Elmendorf AFB, Alaska	43rd TFS	First F-15As received Mar 82
33rd TFW, TAC	Eglin AFB, Florida	58th TFS 59th TFS 60th TFS	To receive F-15C/D during 1984
36th TFW, USAFE	Bitburg AB, W Germany	22nd TFS 53rd TFS 525th TFS	F-15A/B from Dec 76; re-quipped with F-15C/D from Aug 80
49th TFW, TAC	Holloman AFB, New Mexico	7th TFS 8th TFS 9th TFS	Received first F-15A/Bs Oct 77; completely equipped by Apr 78
405th TFW, TAC	Luke AFB, Arizona	426th TFTS 461st TFTS 550th TFTS 555th TFTS	555th was first USAF F-15 squadron, Nov 74
FWW	Nellis AFB, Nevada	422nd TES F-15 FWS	Former 57th FWW/433rd FWS; equipped 76/77
USAFE 17th AF	Soesterberg AB, Netherlands	32nd TFS	F-15A/B late 78; F-15C/D summer 80
ADTAC	Langley AFB, Virginia	48th FIS	Equipped from Aug 81; Det 1 at Tyndall AFB, Florida
ADTAC	McChord AFB, Washington	318th FIS	First F-15 received Jun 83

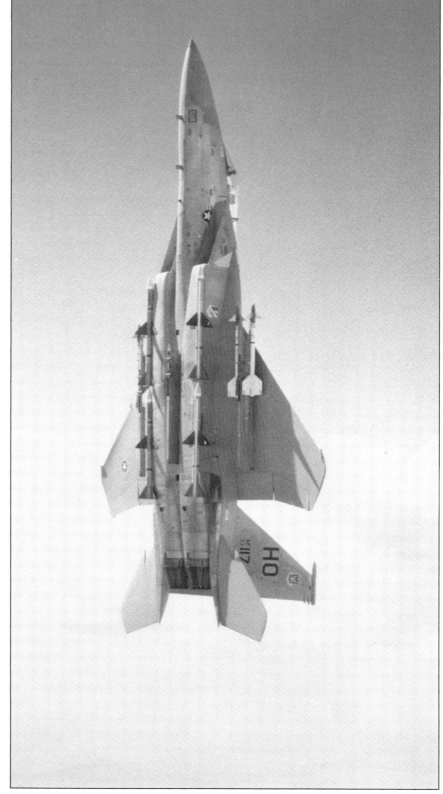

TFS took delivery of its first F-15s during April, the conversion process being successfully concluded during July, by which time Ready Eagle 2 was well under way.

This code name referred to the re-equipment of just one squadron, namely the 32nd TFS at Soesterberg in the Netherlands, and training of air and ground crews began during May 1978. However, since the number of aircraft involved was small, it became necessary for the 1st TFW to cover alert commitments once the F-4E Phantoms previously assigned to the 32nd TFS had departed. Accordingly, exercise Coronet Sandpiper brought the deployment of 18 F-15As on September 13, 1978. These remained in the Netherlands for approximately three months, being manned by 71st TFS pilots for the first 45 days and by members of the 94th TFS for the rest of the deployment. The 1st TFW aircraft were accompanied by the first two F-15As for the 32nd TFS for maintenance training, while the bulk of the F-15s destined for service at Soesterberg followed during November and December 1978, enabling those aircraft involved in Coronet Sandpiper to return home to Langley. By mid-January of 1979 the 32nd TFS was fully equipped and operational with 18 F-15As and a brace of F-15B two-seaters.

Tactical Air Command's fourth F-15 wing was the 33rd TFW which again followed the Ready Team procedure. Stationed at Eglin AFB, Florida, the 33rd was equipped during the first six months of 1979 with sufficient aircraft for just two squadrons, the 58th and 59th TFSs. Shortly afterwards, however, a third squadron, the 60th TFS, was organized to provide training support for the 18th TFW. This was active at Eglin between July 1979 and April 1980 when, with transition of the PACAF (Pacific Air Forces) unit successfully concluded, it deactivated, only to reappear during

1981 with F-15As and F-15Bs made available by the re-equipment of other units.

Flown for the first time in late February 1979, the F-15C was quickly introduced to operational service, with most of the initial production batch joining the 18th TFW at Kadena AB, Okinawa.

Right: An F-15A of the 49th TFW, from Holloman AFB, New Mexico, demonstrates its ability to climb vertically.

Below: Another of Holloman's F-15As. The 49th TFW's three squadrons – the 7th, 8th and 9th TFS – were equipped with Eagles during 1977–78.

Above: 49th TFW F-15As rendezvous with the first KC-10A Extender tanker/transport to be delivered.

PACAF's first, and so far only, F-15 wing entered the transition phase during 1979 and, as already noted, the 60th TFS at Eglin was closely involved in Ready Eagle 3. Highlighted by the successful transpacific deployment of 16 F-15Cs and F-15Ds of the 67th TFS in late September 1979, re-equipment of the 18th TFW was completed in April 1980, other squadrons attached to this wing being the 12th and 44th TFSs.

The conversion of the 18th TFW can essentially be considered as marking the conclusion of the initial phase of Eagle deployment, all subsequent new-production F-15C and D models being used to modernize some of those units which had earlier received F-15As and Bs. Inevitably, this resulted in the appearance of yet another generic

Left: An F-15A of the 33rd TFW, based at Eglin AFB, Florida, sports the unit's distinctive Eagle crest on the inside of its vertical stabilizer.

Below: A 59th TFS, 33rd TFW, F-15A with non-standard serial number marking in formation with Canadian Armed Forces CF-104.

codename – Ready Switch – and began with the 32nd TFS at Soesterberg which disposed of its F-15As and Bs during May and June 1980, replacing them with an identical number of new-build Cs and Ds between May and August of the same year. Attention then shifted to Bitburg's three squadrons which were progressively re-equipped between August 1980 and December 1981, TAC's 1st TFW at Langley was the most recent wing to convert, in a transition programme which began in December 1981 and which was scheduled for completion in mid-1983.

In addition, some F-15Cs and F-15Ds have also been delivered to the 405th Tactical Training Wing, a unit which appeared in August 1979 when it was decided to reorganize training elements at Luke into two separate wings. Consequently, the three F-15 squadrons previously assigned to the 58th TTW split away to form the 405th TTW, leaving the former wing to concentrate mainly on F-4 Phantom crew training. Looking to the future, Eglin's 33rd TFW is due to receive the newer models of the Eagle during 1984.

The substantial numbers of older F-15As and F-15Bs being released by this re-equipment programme have in turn permitted conversion or activation of several other units, one such being the 60th TFS which was organized at Eglin during 1981 and which brought the 33rd TFW up to full strength with three squadrons. Additional training capacity was also made available following the transfer of the 426th TFTS from the 58th TTW to the 405th TTW at Luke and its re-equipment with the F-15.

Perhaps more significant, however, was the opportunity to update those units dedicated solely to the air defence of the continental United States. This process got under way on August. 10, 1981, when the 48th Fighter Interceptor Squadron (FIS) at Langley AFB received its first F-15A for maintenance familiarization training. Previously equipped with the F-106 Delta Dart – a fine interceptor but now fast approaching veteran status – the 48th FIS had taken delivery of half of its planned complement of 20 aircraft by January 1982 and duly attained operational status later in that year. The 48th subsequently joined four other F-15 units taking part in the William Tell air defence weapons meet at Tyndall AFB, Florida, in October. Despite this being the Eagle's first participation in the event, the type generally performed well, with Kadena's 18th TFW fighting off the challenge posed by F-4, F-101 and F-106 interceptor squadrons to win the overall competition.

ADTAC's (Air Defense Tactical Air Command) four remaining F-106 squadrons – the 5th, 49th, 87th and 318th FISs at Minot, Griffiss, Sawyer and McChord AFBs respectively – were all expected to convert to the F-15 in the next two or three years, and the 318th received its first Eagle on June 10, 1983. The type was also scheduled to equip ADTAC's Air Defense Weapons Center at Tyndall.

One other unit also benefited from the availability of early model Eagles, this being the Elmendorf-based 43rd TFS which took delivery of its first examples on March 1, 1982 and which is now fully equipped with 27 F-15As and F-15Bs. Tasked with the air defence of Alaska and the approaches to the northern United States, the 43rd TFS forms part of the 21st TFW. As well as conducting operations from Elmendorf also maintains alert detachments at Eielson AFB, Galena Air Force Station and King Salmon Airport.

No survey of USAF Eagle operations would be complete without some mention of the 57th Fighter Weapons Wing at Nellis, which played a major part in bringing the F-15 to full operational status. More recently known as the 57th TTW, this unit is principally concerned with test and evaluation of weapons systems and the formulation of the best tactics for their use. Accordingly, it features examples of most of the major tactical aircraft types in the USAF inventory. The 57th took delivery of its first F-15s during 1976, these joining the 433rd Fighter Weapons Squadron (FWS), initially for the AIMVAL/ACEVAL project and in later years for the refinement of tactics. A further influx of F-15s in 1977 permitted some to be assigned to the 422nd FWS for follow-on operational test and evaluation work but the Nellis-based unit has recently undergone a major reorganization which has seen the disappearance of

Right: The three squadrons of the 36th TFW traded in their F-15As and Bs for C (shown) and D models starting in August 1980.

Below: Two F-15As of ADTAC's Langley-based 48th FIS retract their landing gear following a formation takeoff in October 1982.

Above left: A pair of 18th TFW F-15Cs over the Pacific. The 18th is PACAF's only Eagle unit.

Above: An F-15C of the Soesterberg-based 32nd TFS, which transferred to the newer model in mid-1980.

these two squadrons and their replacement by the F-15 Division of the Fighter Weapons School and the 422nd Tactical Evaluation Squadron (TES) respectively. Despite these changes in nomenclature, the work performed at Nellis remains essentially the same.

Following the Eagle's introduction to operational service in November 1974, the next three years or so were essentially a period of consolidation. It was not until early in 1978 that the F-15 really began to flex its wings, when, in Operation Condor, eight aircraft from the 1st TFW flew to Osan AB, Korea. This was the first overseas deployment by a US-based F-15 wing and one which involved local exercises with PACAF and RoKAF (Republic of Korea Air Force) elements.

As already noted, Coronet Sandpiper brought 18 of the 1st TFW's F-15s to Soesterberg in the last three months of 1978 to cover the 32nd TFS's 'Zulu' alert commitment while that unit converted to the Eagle, and the new year celebrations were barely over before the 1st TFW took to the road again. A detachment of 12 aircraft headed for Saudi Arabia on January 13 and spent ten days overseas during which time operations were conducted from several Saudi air bases including Khamis Mushayt, now one of three RSAF (Royal Saudi Air Force) F-15 operating locations. In addition to overseas visits, the 1st TFW was a regular participant in Red Flag manoeuvres at Nellis and also headed north to Canada to participate in Maple Flag during April and May 1980. The latter is a similar exercise although it is predicated more upon a European environment, a scenario which is greatly helped by the striking resemblance of the local terrain to that of Europe.

Further deployments in 1980 saw 12 aircraft from Kadena's 18th TFW visit Kwang-Ju AB in Korea during March for Team Spirit '80, a simulated combat exercise against RoKAF and other USAF elements. Team Spirit now appears to be an annual endeavour for the 18th TFW, as many as 24 aircraft taking part in 1981 and 1982. Also in 1980, the 33rd TFW took some of its Eagles overseas for the first time when 18 flew to Bremgarten in West Germany. Code-named Coronet Barrel and running from October 3 to November 5, this exercise, like others of the Coronet series, was intended to provide aircrew with experience of the area in which they may at some future date be required to fly and fight.

Multiple deployments

For the 49th TFW, 1981 was a particularly memorable year. The months of August and September were dominated by no less than three Coronet deployments – to Jever and Lahr in West Germany and to Aalborg in Denmark – each of which involved 12 F-15s. Meanwhile, the 1st TFW returned to Europe in May 1982 after an absence of more than three years when, in a split exercise, they conducted two back-to-back visits to the Netherlands. The first of these, Coronet Sidewinder I, brought F-15s to Gilze-Rijen between May 17 and June 4, and was followed on June 7 by Coronet Sidewinder II, in which 12 more aircraft visited Soesterberg for a stay lasting 15 days.

Later in the same year, as part of the regular autumn NATO exercises, virtually half of the 33rd TFW flew to West Germany under the Crested Cap dual-based commitment; they stayed for almost a month, with 24 Eagles going to Bremgarten and a further 12 to Sollingen. However, perhaps the most remarkable demonstration of mobility during 1982 was the deployment of six F-15Cs of the 18th TFW from Kadena to Florida at the beginning of October. The record-breaking 7,000 mile (9,620km) ferry flight accomplished non-stop in 15

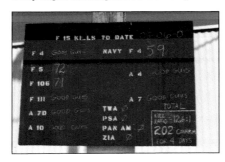

Above: The scoreboard for a Red Flag exercise held at Nellis AFB, Nevada, in May and June, 1980.

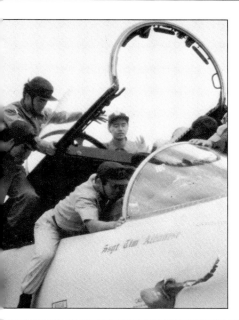

Opposite, top: AIM-7 Sparrow missiles are brought out to arm a 36th TFW F-15C during the William Tell 82 weapons meet.

Left: Demonstration of rescue methods for Japanese ground crew during a deployment to Nyutabaru AB as part of Exercise Cope North 81-3.

Below: An F-15C of the 18th TFW is the centre of attention after flying from Okinawa to Florida for the William Tell 82 meet.

Right, top to bottom: The 38th TFW's F-15Cs followed their non-stop 7,000-mile (9,620km) flight by taking first place in the William Tell meet at Tyndall AFB. This sequence shows one of the unit's six Eagles, armed with Sidewinders but no Sparrows, scrambling to an interception.

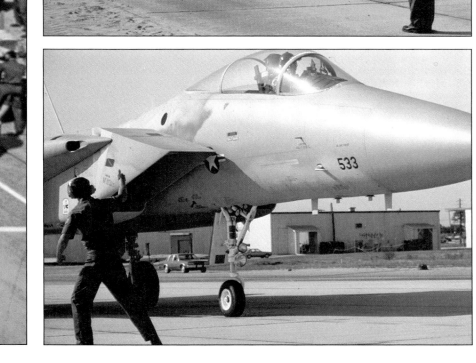

hours, with aerial refuelling and other support was furnished largely by just one KC-10A Extender from the Douglas side of the McDonnell Douglas Corporation. Each of the six Eagles was refuelled no less than ten times during this epic flight, the accompanying KC-10A itself receiving fuel three times from another Extender and some KC-135A Stratotankers. Arriving at Eglin in good shape, five of the six F-15Cs subsequently made the short hop to Tyndall where they participated in the William Tell 82 weapons meet, providing further proof of the type's capability by emerging as the overall winners of this air defence competition.

Eagle exports

By mid-1983 the only export customers for the Eagle were Israel, Japan and Saudi Arabia. Israel was the first to receive Eagles when it accepted a batch of three aircraft on December 10, 1976, these plus one other of the initial order for 25 aircraft (23 F-15As and two F-15Bs), being reconditioned USAF evaluation machines. More recently, a further 15 Eagles, almost certainly F-15Cs were delivered to the Israeli Defence Force – Air Force (IDFAF) and another 11 are known to be on order although these are currently embargoed as a result of Israel's adventures in Lebanon.

As far as operating units and bases are concerned, Israel has maintained its usual near-impenetrable degree of secrecy although numerous reports indicate that No 133 Squadron was the first IDFAF squadron to equip with the F-15.

Almost inevitably, Israel became the first to utilize the Eagle in combat. Although, again, relatively little first-hand information has been forthcoming, it is known that the F-15 has performed most satisfactorily. It was first committed to action in late June 1979 against a sizeable force of Syrian MiG-21s, six of which were apparently destroyed by six F-15s and two Kfirs. All types of primary ordnance – AIM-7 Sparrow, AIM-9 Sidewinder and M61 Vulcan 20mm gun – were used in achieving these successes. Further kills followed in September, when four MiG-21s were destroyed in an abortive Syrian attempt to down an IDFAF RF-4E Phantom engaged on reconnaissance duties. More recently, at least one Syrian MiG-23 has fallen to Israeli Eagles over Lebanon, and it is interesting to note that IDFAF pilots do not seem unduly concerned about degraded-system operation. Combat is usualy conducted at close quarters with infra-red homing missiles and, of course, the 20mm cannon, underlining the continuing requirement for the classic dogfighting type of aircraft.

Japan selected the Eagle to be its fourth-generation interceptor during December 1976, after a lengthy evaluation which initially considered no less than 13 potential candidates. The seven still in contention by 1975 comprised the Viggen, Tornado, Mirage F1, F-14 Tomcat, F-15 Eagle, F-16 Fighting Falcon and F/A-18 Hornet. These were

reduced to just three – the F-14, F-15 and F-16 – in January 1976, and further detailed studies during the summer of that year finally resulted in the decision that a derivative of the Eagle known as the F-15J was best suited to Japan's peculiar defence requirements.

Initial plans anticipated the acquisition of 123 Eagles for service with five squadrons, but this figure was later cut to exactly 100, comprising 88 F-15J single-seaters and 12 F-15DJ two-seaters. Two of the F-15Js and all of the F-15DJs were to be manufactured by the parent company in St. Louis, Missouri. The remaining 86 F-15Js will be built by Mitsubishi Heavy Industries at Komaki, the first eight from knocked-down assemblies provided by MCAIR.

Japanese service

With the type still in the early stages of its operational career with the JASDF (Japan Air Self-Defense Force), plans current in June 1983 anticipated an ultimate total of four squadrons operating Eagles by 1986. Flying for the first time on June 4, 1980, the first F-15J was formally handed over to JASDF representatives at St Louis on July 15. It then went to Luke AFB where, in company with F-15J number two, it spent several months on weapons firing trials and other tasks, and it was not until March 1981 that these two aircraft became the first JASDF Eagles to fly in Japan. Both joined the Air Proving Wing at Gifu AB for further evaluation and test work, and they were later joined at Gifu by some Mitsubishi-built examples and a few of the two-seat F-15DJs.

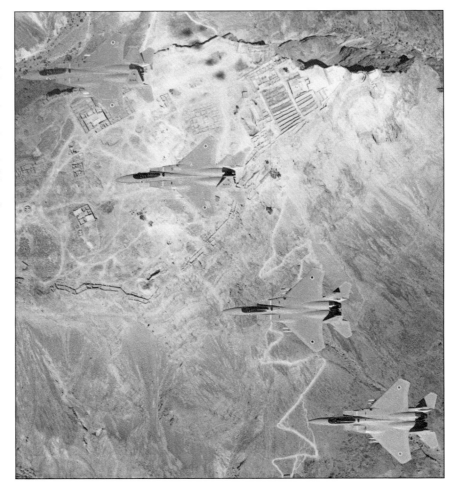

The first Komaki-assembled F-15J made its maiden flight on August 19, 1981 and was eventually delivered to the JASDF during December, in time for the formation of the F-15 Temporal Squadron at Nyutabaru AB on January 1, 1982. This unit was equipped with a handful of F-15Js and F-15DJs and tasked with initial conversion training duties. Formal training of JASDF pilots actually began several months earlier at Luke AFB, Arizona, under the aegis of the 555th TFTS, which temporarily operated at least four of the F-15DJs in full USAF insignia. The F-15 Temporal Squadron lasted only three months before metamorphosing into No 202 Squadron at the same base on April 1, 1982 and operating subsequently as part of No 5 Air Wing.

By the end of 1982 production at Mitsubishi's Komaki Factory was beginning to pick up, some 13 F-15Js having been completed and flown with most of these going to No 202 Squadron. The next phase of service introduction was scheduled to begin in 1983. No 203 Squadron at Chitose AB near Sapporo was the second JASDF unit to receive Eagles, followed in 1984 by No 204 Squadron at Nyutabaru. Chitose is also expected to be the home of a fourth squadron in Fiscal Year 1985 (April 1985–March 1986), and it seems likely that procurement of up to 50 additional

Above: A Royal Saudi Air Force F-15C armed with Sidewinders flies in formation with one of the Lightning interceptors it has now replaced with No 13 Fighter Squadron.

aircraft will eventually permit the formation of at least two more squadrons in the late 1980s.

The third customer for the Eagle is Saudi Arabia which has contracted for a total of 62 aircraft comprising 47 F-15Cs and 15 F-15Ds. Because one of the stipulations of the 'Camp David' agreement lays down that no more than 60 Eagles may be present in Saudi Arabia at any give time, two of the single-seat F-15Cs are to be held in the United States as attrition replacements.

Deliveries to the Royal Saudi Air Force (RSAF) actually began during January 1981 although, again, a small number of aircraft initially went to Luke AFB for pilot training under the 555th TFTS and like the Japanese examples these were operated in full USAF insignia while at Luke. RSAF Eagles began to reach Saudi Arabia during 1982, and by the end of that year a total of 47 had been delivered, with the balance due to be handed over by the summer of 1983. Details of actual service use are scarce but it is thought that No 13 Squadron, previously equipped with the Lightning, is the first F-15 unit, and that three air bases – at Dhahran, Khamis Mushayt and Taif – will support F-15 operations. It therefore seems reasonable to assume that each will host one squadron of about 20 aircraft. Their primary task is air defence.

Above: The first of a total of 86 single-seat F-15Js to be licence-built by Mitsubishi, supplementing the two MCAIR-built single-seaters and ten F-15DJs, also supplied by the St Louis company.

Above: One of the 15 F-15Ds which Saudi Arabia has bought along with 47 single-seaters.

Above: Israeli deployment is shrouded in secrecy, but it is known that the country's initial order for 25 F-15A and B Eagles went to equip No 133 Squadron of the IDF-AF.

Below: One of the two MCAIR-built F-15J Eagles arrives at Gifu air base in Japan after a ferry flight from St Louis.

Performance and Handling

One of the fundamental aims of the FX programme was to produce a fighter capable of out-performing any actual or potential Warsaw Pact opponent, though there was considerable debate over the precise details of how this was to be defined. With its unprecedentedly high thrust-to-weight ratio and low wing loading for maximum manoeuvrability, the Eagle has demonstrated the required level of performance, and its handling qualities at speeds ranging from 100 knots to Mach 2.5 have won unqualified praise from pilots as well as providing a thrilling spectacle for air show audiences.

The performance requirements embodied in the FX Request for Proposals were intended to equip the resulting fighter to better all existing and projected Warsaw Pact opponents. As of the late 1960s these were represented by the small, agile MiG-21 and the rather bigger but highly manoeuvrable MiG-23, expected to be encountered at all altitudes; the fast, high-altitude MiG-25; and the Su-15 interceptor, for which the look-down radar capability was likely to be needed.

At the same time, some compromises had to be accepted, so that the USAF's original requirement for a maximum speed of Mach 2.7 at high altitudes, for example, was reduced to Mach 2.3, with a Mach 2.5 minimum burst capability. The higher speed would not only have prevented the use of a bubble canopy, added up to 3,000lb (1,360kg) to gross weight and reduced dash radius, it would also use up fuel at a rate of 65,000lb/hr (29,480kg/hr), equivalent to consuming the entire internal fuel load of an F-15A in about 11 minutes. The fuel flow at Mach 2.3 was estimated at a significantly lower 45,000lb/hr (20,400kg/hr). It was also argued that higher speeds were in any case irrelevant to most missions.

Other performance figures specified included a top speed of Mach 1.2 at sea level, which it was felt would provide a useful margin of superiority over potential opponents. The wing was to be optimized for buffet-free performance at Mach 0.9 and 30,000ft (9,100m). More generally, performance was to be a consequence of high thrust-to-weight ratio and low wing loading, which had been recognized as the fundamental elements in providing the desired degree of superiority in performance and agility.

Wing loading

In its production form, at a takeoff weight of 41,500lb (18,820kg) with full internal fuel, the F-15A's 608sq ft (56.5sq m) of wing area gives a loading figure of just over 68lb/sq ft (333kg/sq m), and with half internal fuel this figure falls to 57lb/sq ft (279kg/sq m). Similarly, thrust-to-weight ratio at takeoff, with the F100s in full afterburner and full internal fuel, is 1.15:1, and by the time half the fuel has been used the ratio increases to nearly 1.4:1. By comparison, wing load-

ing of the F-4E at combat weight is 80lb/sq ft (390kg/sq m), with a thrust-to-weight ratio of approximately 0.85:1.

When translated into actual flying qualities these figures have important consequences. The four forces acting on an aircraft in flight are thrust, drag, weight and lift, and all are inter-related. Lift and drag increase as airspeed rises; both lift and drag are increased by increasing the angle of attack, and increasing the angle of bank in a turn also increases drag. Lift is considered as acting perpendicularly to the surface of a wing, and in a steep turn it has to counteract both the weight of the aircraft and the centrifugal force acting on it. Lift can be increased by increasing the angle of attack, but this also results in more drag, which in turn demands more power if the turn is to be sustained.

It is in this context that the theories of former fighter instructor Major John Boyd assume such importance. By the time Boyd was assigned to the FX programme in October 1966 he had already developed his theory of energy manoeuvrability in conjunction with Tom Christie, a mathematician working

Above: The F-15's thrust-to-weight ratio is such that it can accelerate in a vertical climb to supersonic speeds – the first fighter to do so.

at Eglin AFB. By subtracting drag from thrust and multiplying the residue by velocity, Boyd realized, it was possible to express the 'energy rate': when drag exceeds thrust the energy rate becomes negative, so that either more thrust must be made available or the aircraft will lose altitude, airspeed or both. This in turn gives rise to the concept of specific excess power (Ps), or the amount of 'spare' thrust available in a turn, and explains the importance of the F-15's unprecedentedly high thrust-to-weight ratio.

Wing loading also has an important effect on turning performance. As an aircraft banks, the amount of life needed to counteract the combination of gravity and centrifugal force increases as the bank angle increases; and since the

Below: A 32nd TFS F-15A leaves the Camp New Amsterdam runway at a speed of 135kt after a takeoff run of only 900ft (274m).

radius of turn at a given airspeed depends on the bank angle, it follows that the turn radius of which an aircraft is capable is dependent on the extent to which it can continue to develop lift with increasing bank angles. The high available thrust enables the Eagle to maintain or increase speeds in high banked turns, thus enabling it to fly turns at high rates. Thus the F-15's low wing loading and high thrust-to-weight ratio combine to make it exceptionally manoeuvrable. Compared with the F-4, the F-15 can take off in a shorter distance, accelerate faster to a higher maximum speed, turn with a reduced radius and at a higher

rate and fly higher; alternatively, it can climb at a lower airspeed.

To allow pilots to make maximum use of the Eagle's power and agility a dual flight control system was developed. The conventional hydromechanical system operates through push rod linkages acting on the valves of hydraulic actuators which deflect the control surfaces. The pitch-roll control assembly is a mechanical system which modifies the response of the system and the aileron-rudder interconnect couples the rudders and stabilators so that the former are operated automatically in conjunction with the stabilators, allowing ma-

noeuvres to be carried out using the stick alone.

Meanwhile, the automatic control augmentation system (CAS) forms a separate fly-by-wire system using electrical signal signals and servo motors to operate the hydraulic actuators. The CAS system includes pitch and yaw rate, angle of attack and dynamic pressure sensors, as well as accelerometers to monitor vertical and lateral acceleration. It is thus able to compute the correct settings for the control surfaces at any combination of speed and g forces.

The CAS also senses the stick forces

Above: A 36th TFW F-15A in formation with an F-5E in the blue-grey camouflage of an Aggressor squadron. The Aggressors simulate MiG-21s for combat training.

applied by the pilot, translating them into electrical signals to the control surface actuators: should the mechanical system fail the CAS would continue to operate the control surfaces. For

Below: Even with a full load of three external tanks, the F-15 is capable of impressive takeoff performance and rapid climb.

Above: Three 405th TTW F-15As in a steep climb over the Arizona desert with engines in full afterburner delivering 11 tons of thrust each.

Right: Performance envelope of the Strike Eagle ground-attack version of the F-15 remains impressive even with external stores.

safety, the CAS is a dual-channel system in which the signals carried by each channel are continuously compared with each other, and if an error greater than a predetermined maximum is detected both are automatically disengaged. The Eagle can be manoeuvred with the CAS off using the mechanical system alone: in this mode, control is reportedly equal to that of earlier fighters, with the CAS providing a marked improvement in handling and effectively intervening to point the aircraft in whatever direction the stick is moved.

The control surfaces themselves are straightforward. The all-moving stabilators act in unison for pitch control and differentially for roll control in conjunction with the ailerons. Being mounted outside the engines, the stabilators could be positioned out of the wing wake without interference from the jet efflux, and at high angles of attack, when the ailerons become progressively less effective, the tail surfaces generate all required roll moments. The twin vertical stabilizers are tall enough to maintain stability at high angles of attack, and the twin booms on which the tail surfaces are mounted are braced to each other via the titanium engine bay assembly to provide a rigid structure for transferring the torsional

loads from the tail to the aircraft.

Modifications to the aerodynamic configuration and control system as a result of flight testing are described in detail in the first chapter. Structural alterations included the clipping of the wingtips to reduce buffeting at high subsonic speeds and high g at around 30,000ft (9,100m); the increased chord on the outer sections of the stabilators to eliminate flutter, producing the notched leading edges of these surfaces; and the doubling in size of the speedbrake.

At the same time, several changes were made to the flight control system, such as the reduction in stick control forces during high-g manoeuvring to make CAS-off control easier. The CAS itself was modified to be less responsive to small, sharp stick deflections, since its original bias towards rapid rolling made the aircraft's response alarmingly jerky during more precise manoeuvres such as formation flying, air-to-air refuelling and target tracking with the gun. Similarly, the aileron-rudder interconnect system was made to disconnect on touch-down to eliminate the accentu-

Right: The F-15 has demonstrated an ability to turn well inside an F-4E, or climb 7,100ft (2,164m) while matching the Phantom's tightest level turn.

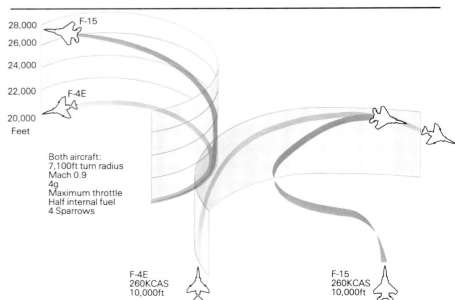

Both aircraft:
7,100ft turn radius
Mach 0.9
4g
Maximum throttle
Half internal fuel
4 Sparrows

F-4E
260KCAS
10,000ft

F-15
260KCAS
10,000ft

Above: Superb performance is matched by a magnificent view from the cockpit: a 49th TFW F-15A is in the background.

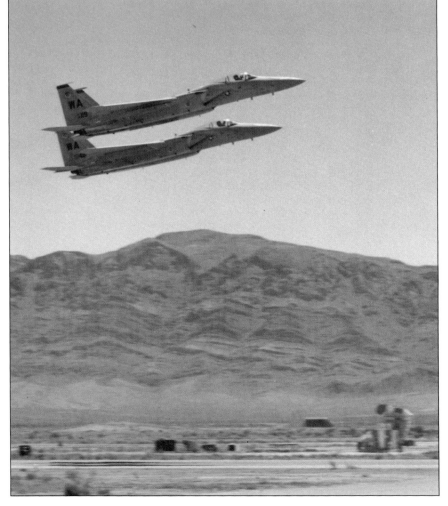

Left: A pair of 57th FWW Eagles demonstrate the type's excellent low-level handling qualities over Nellis AFB, Arizona.

ation of weathervaning during cross-wind landings.

While all these problems were being identified and corrected during the flight test programme, the new fighter was demonstrated to a number of journalists during 1974. Clark Martin, of the US journal *Aviation Week and Space Technology*, flew in an F-15B when the aircraft was still subject to a limit of +5.9g: the left afterburner failed to ignite until after liftoff, but the takeoff was still impressive, a 3,300ft (1,000m) ground roll taking 18 seconds to a liftoff speed of 175kt. This compares with a ground roll of only 900ft (274m) for a production single-seater in standard interceptor configuration, when the nose-wheel is rotated at around 100kt and liftoff takes place at 135kt.

Following liftoff the F-15B went into a 50deg climb at 300kt, reaching a height of 14,000ft (4,267m) by the time it was over the end of the 15,000ft (4,572m) runway. During subsequent manoeuvres Clark reported that CAS-off flight was equal to that of earlier fighters, enabling tracking manoeuvres at up to 4g to be carried out at 10,000ft (3,000m) and 350kt. Climb and acceleration were also demonstrated, with a climb at better than 6,000ft/min (1,800m/min) in Military (non-afterburning) power to 32,000ft (9,750m) followed by

acceleration in full afterburner from Mach 0.9 to Mach 1.1 in 10 seconds and Mach 1.2 in 20 seconds.

Another close observer of an early demonstration flight was Captain Robert J. Hoag, Editor of the USAF *Fighter Weapons Review*. Following in an F-4 chase plane, Captain Hoag watched the Eagle lift off after a ground roll of 1,200ft (366m) and reach 10,000ft (3,000m) over a ground track of less than 5,000ft (1,500m). To compare the turning performance of the two aircraft, the F-4 initiated a 5½g turn in full afterburner, starting from a speed of 350-400kt and at an altitude of 12,000ft (3,650m). The Eagle, starting at the same speed and altitude and at a slant range of 6,000ft (1,830m) was able to close to a minimum range on the Phantom's tail within 540deg of turn, using only military power and with no trace of the severe buffeting experienced by the F-4.

Another manoeuvre which particularly impressed Captain Hoag, who was moved to describe the F-15 as a "Superfighter", was a transition from 110kt flight, with landing gear and flaps down, to an Immelmann in full afterburner with gear and flaps up. The transition was immediate, and the Eagle was able to accelerate throughout the manoeuvre.

The implications for combat of the

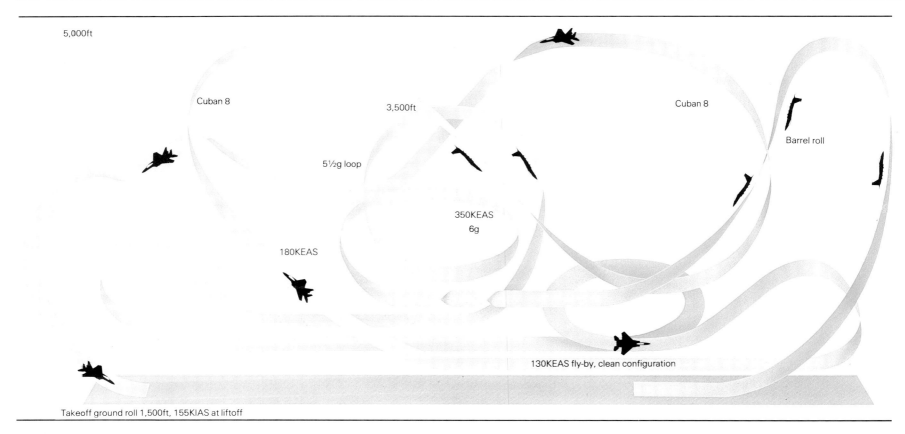

5,000ft

Cuban 8

3,500ft

Cuban 8

Barrel roll

5½g loop

350KEAS
6g

180KEAS

130KEAS fly-by, clean configuration

Takeoff ground roll 1,500ft, 155KIAS at liftoff

Above: Fair-weather flying display given by the Strike Eagle during its public premiere at the 1982 Farnborough Air Show.

power implicit in such demonstrations are obvious. While the Eagle should be able to accelerate out of trouble fairly easily, an opponent would find it extremely hard to get away. The F-15's ability to maintain controllable flight over a wide range of speeds and at angles of attack up to 26deg can enhance the effectiveness of both missiles and guns. And the ability to maintain acceleration at steep angles is a significant advantage against the high-speed, high-altitude MiG-25, allowing the target to be tracked by the radar against a clutter-free background in a snap-up intercept.

Overall, the Eagle's air combat superiority is directly attributable to the high lift and excess power specified in the original requirement. Whereas the pilot of an F-4 must be aware of the need to conserve energy, and will often have to build up energy in combat by diving away into a zoom climb, the F-15 has so much power available that it can accelerate straight into high-g ma-

Below: 36th TFW F-15A touches down with airbrake at full 45deg extension. Early control problems on the rollout were corrected by modifications to the control system.

noeuvres, and sustain them for long periods without losing altitude or airspeed.

Of course, there are other requirements in combat than pure power and manoeuvrability: above all, the pilot must be able to use them effectively. In this respect the bubble canopy and the exceptional visibility it provides is of fundamental importance – according to Captain Hoag, "The pilot feels as if he is riding astride the bird, rather than in it". There is also room for him to twist around in his seat without banging his head against the canopy.

Cockpit layout
The cockpit layout itself was given an enthusiastic welcome. The most frequently used controls are positioned at the top of the centre instrument panel (HUD, UHF radio, Mode 3 IFF and position identification) or on the left console near the throttle (radar controls, fuel jettison, ILS TACAN, landing lights, BIT control panel auxiliary radio and master IFF). Other instruments on the front panel include the air-to-air and air-to-ground weapons monitoring systems, the radar display, standard flight instruments and engine instruments. The right console contains the engine controls, INS control panel and environmental controls. Altogether there are 30 per cent fewer gauges than in an F-4 cockpit, and with the HUD acting as the primary source of flight information and

the communications controls located just below it the time spent looking inside the cockpit is reduced to a minimum.

The pilot is further helped to keep his head up by the location of the main weapon and radar controls on the stick and throttle. With the CAS translating the pilot's inputs into electrical signals, finger and thumb pressure on the stick

Below: Touchdown by a 555th TFS Eagle. Even without a brake parachute the F-15 needs a shorter landing run than the F-4.

is enough to maintain control, while the controls for a number of other functions are also carried on the stick. A trim button allows the aircraft's attitude to be adjusted in pitch or yaw axes; the trigger engages the HUD camera and fires the gun; the weapon release button, depending on the mode selected, will engage the HUD camera, launch a selected missile, release bombs, designate a target or illuminate a target for a Sparrow; another button uncages or cages the seeker heads of heat-seeking Sidewinders or laser-guided bombs; and the air refuelling receptacle re-

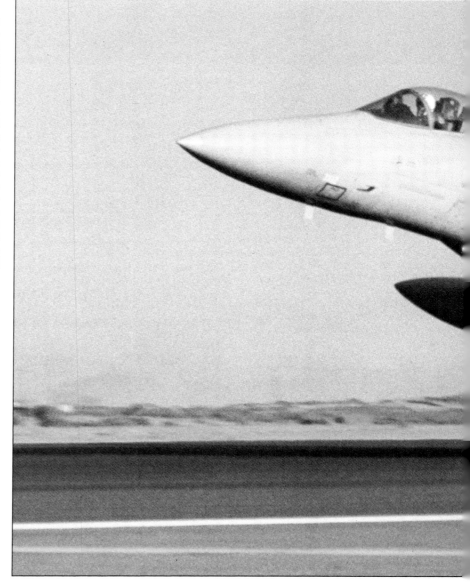

lease switch, when the radar is engaged, enables the pilot to engage the radar's boresight or super-search modes. The former commands the radar to scan directly ahead and lock on the first target it detects within ten miles (16km), while in super-search the radar scans the 20deg HUD field of view up to ten miles ahead and locks on any target detected, displaying a box in the HUD to indicate its position to the pilot.

The throttles also carry a variety of controls. Apart from the microphone and IFF transmitter, there is an ECM dispenser switch for releasing chaff or flares, a weapon mode selector for the air-to-air radar mode appropriate to gun, Sparrow or Sidewinder, and the speedbrake control, plus more radar controls. The antenna elevation control allows the radar scan pattern to be adjusted up or down, while the target designator control adjusts the position of the radar scope target acquisition gate, used to designate a target detected in normal search modes.

HOTAS philosophy
The thinking behind the head-up HOTAS (hands on throttle and stick) system of combat is summed up succinctly by Colonel Wendell H. Shawler, Director of the F-15 Joint Test Force, 1973–76: "Everything you need is on the throttle and stick". However, he adds that these functions need to be simplified to avoid confusion during the heat of battle. According to Jack Cranes of MCAIR, addressing the Society of Experimental Test Pilots on the F/A-18 HOTAS system, the average pilot can only use three functions intelligently, wisely and properly. Air-to-air weapon selection on the F-15 is split into three functions: gun, Sidewinder or Sparrow.

Again according to Colonel Shawler, on selecting guns, "you automatically got everything up there (in the HUD)

Right: 36th TFW F-15Cs practise a formation takeoff from a West German autobahn. Nose-up normally takes place when the Eagle reaches a speed of 100kt.

you needed for guns, including short-range radar on your radar selection". The same applies to the two types of AAM. "The fact that you were selecting one of three functions – you got everything you needed. You couldn't do much else – you don't want to. When you start getting all these complexities where you put 50 functions on the stick and throttle, if you select one thing over here, you get three choices there, it gets very difficult." During Colonel Shawler's time HOTAS did not strain the pilot's workload; but later, when all the ECM and EW aspects were added to the one-man cockpit, it did, in his opinion, "put the workload over a lot of people's capabilities".

This view has been echoed by at least one experienced F-15 pilot, Major Dito Ladd, who until transferring to the 527th Aggressors was Chief of Weapons and Tactics with the 525th TFS, 36th TFW. In May 1983 Major Ladd recalled: "There are times when you feel like 'Yeah, I've got this thing whipped, I can take advantage of every opportunity the weapon provides.' That was generally after a period of intense flying. Flying once a day or twice a day over a period of two to three weeks there are times when the airplane can be fun, with one man it can be extremely effective, but it take the time and practice to do it. It's just like anything, you've got to practice."

Right: Two F-15Cs of the 18th TFW take off at sunset from Kwang-Ju air base, Republic of Korea, in April 1982 during one of PACAF's annual Team Spirit exercises.

Future Variants

Although intended purely as an air-superiority fighter, the Eagle has proved a ready convert to the ground-attack role, and the manufacturer's Strike Eagle demonstrator has paved the way for a potential dual-role derivative. In addition, the type's rapid acceleration to high altitudes made it the obvious candidate as launch vehicle for the USAF's new anti-satellite missile, and other proposed variants include tactical reconnaissance and defence-suppression replacements for the RF-4C and F-4G Wild Weasel versions of the venerable Phantom.

By 1983 the F-15 Eagle had progressed through three distinct phases. The first was its development to the F-15A production fighter, designed primarily for air superiority, but with a secondary ground attack capability. Phase two was to increase the internal fuel capacity (and thus the maximum takeoff weight)m offer provisions for conformal tanks, and add a programmable signal processor to the radar system, to produce the F-15C and two-seat F-15D. The current Multi-stage Improvement Plan (MSIP) for the F-15C/D will offer provision for the AIM-120 AMRAAM, improved ECM and C^3 (command, control and communications) systems, a programmable armament control system, enhanced radar and an improved internal computer.

The next version to appear, the F-15E, was originally known by the manufacturers as Strike Eagle and was,

in effect, a dual-role fighter offering improved weapons system flexibility and avionics/radar performance in the ground attack role without sacrificing its proven air-to-air capability. The first public demonstration of the new model was its appearance at the Farnborough Air Show in September 1980. The Strike Eagle, a converted F-15B flown for the first time in its new configuration on July 8, 1980, was a private venture by MCAIR and their subcontractors. It featured the extra underwing pylons, provision for the FAST pack conformal

Above: Dive-bombing demonstration by the second development F-15B, 71-0291, in its Strike Eagle configuration in 1980.

tanks and the developed APG-63 radar with SAR techniques, and its projected role was that of an all-weather interdiction aircraft to supplement, and later replace, the remaining F-111s in the TAC inventory.

The key to the Strike Eagle's expanded capabilities lay in the improvements to the radar and avionics. In essence, these advances make it possible to use the radar more intelligently with the aid of PSP (programmable signal processing). Taking advantage of the aircraft's forward speed to give real-time ground mapping, it is possible to achieve much better resolution, allowing the radar to be operated on a time-share basis between the three separate

Below: Strike Eagle demonstrates its ability to carry a heavy load of Mk 20 Rockeye cluster bomb dispensers – plus four Sidewinders – in 1981.

Left: Among the weapons carried by the Strike Eagle company-funded demonstrator were the Matra Durandal anti-runway weapon.

Above: Command and status, tactical situation, radar, and duplicate of the pilot's HUD displays dominate the aft cockpit of the F-15 AFCD.

Left: Strike Eagle carries out a simulated ground attack with the General Electric 30mm gun pod over Wisconsin in 1980.

modes of terrain-following and avoidance, ground-mapping and air search. Based on a two-seat F-15B, the Strike Eagle carries a second crew member to manage the increased number of avionics systems, which could also include FLIR and LANTIRN.

The USAF were impressed with the Strike Eagle and its potential, especially as the air-to-air capabilities are not impaired by the air-to-ground enhancements. Although a new Advanced Tactical Fighter was planned for the 1990s, there was a requirement for 398 dual-role fighters to enter service in the mid-1980s. To this end, a comparable evaluation in 1982–83 examined the enhanced capabilities of both the F-15 and the delta-winged F-16XL. The projected F-15E would have terrain avoidance built in to its radar and linked to a radar altimeter, but despite being little more than a software change, automatic terrain-following using the LANTIRN system is only considered as a growth option. Some of the USAF's mission requirements would require an F-15E to

Above: In its new guise of dual-role fighter demonstrator, 71-0291 carries 22 Mk 20 Rockeyes over St Louis in May 1983.

penetrate to the target by night and in bad weather at around 500ft (150m), using FLIR for target identification and delivering its weapons with the possible assistance of a laser designator, which MCAIR consider calls for a two-man crew.

During the six-month trial at Edwards AFB, Californ.a, more than 200 test

Below: Formation takeoff from Lambert-St Louis, home of MCAIR, with the F-15 dual-role demonstrator in the foreground.

flights were conducted. During the evaluation, the four aircraft demonstrated their capabilities in a number of areas: long-range, all-environment radar; extended flying range and increased payload; high-speed, low-altitude missions; improved survivability; accurate weapons release; and a two-man crew configuration. As an indication of the increase in payload and range performance, MCAIR quote a 7,000lb (3,175kg) increase in take-off weight to 75,000lb (34,020kg). Another F-15, equipped with conformal tanks,

three drop tanks and eight 500lb (227kg) Mk 82 bombs, demonstrated long range combined with a dual air-to-air and air-to-ground role, while 16 differing stores configurations were flight tested on the Eagle's five pylons and four semi-recessed missile stations.

The Eagle evaluation, which began on November 1, 1982, and was concluded on April 30, 1983, used four aircraft. The F-15B Advanced Fighter Capability Demonstrator (formerly Strike Eagle), with the specially-equipped rear cockpit, APG-63 radar with

SAR capability and the Ford Aerospace Pave Tack FLIR laser pod, flew 66 sorties and notched up 121·1 hours; an F-15C with conformal tanks and weapons adapters to increase number of the air-to-ground weapons pylons from three to five flew 104 hours in 50 sorties; and two F-15Ds, one of which was equipped with the Ford Aerospace/Texas Instruments FLIR and laser tracker/marker pod, made a combined total of 88 flights, involving nearly 130 hours in the air. Advanced rear cockpits equipped with four multi-pur-

Left: The Advanced Fighter Capability Demonstrator equipped with bombs, Sidewinders, forward-looking infra-red pod and long-range ground-mapping radar takes off from Eglin AFB, Florida.

Above: The MCAIR Strike Eagle in its original form, before conversion to AFCD and dual-role demonstrator for USAF trials.

pose video screens allowed the occupant to control the various radar, navigation and communications displays simultaneously, and the Eagle successfully completed USAF flight requirements for carrying the 500lb (227kg) Mk 82 and 2000lb (907kg) Mk 84 bombs, BDU-38 and CBU-58 weapons. MCAIR officials are quoted as saying the F-15s "achieved accurate visual and radar weapons delivery" during the trials.

Relating some of these claims to sample mission profiles, an F-15C with conformal tanks plus one centreline

tank could take off from a base in the south of the Sinai peninsula and conduct a hi-lo-lo-hi mission, including a 50nm dash at Mach 0·9, to attack a target in the extreme north of Greece with 12 Mk 20 Rockeye bombs. Alternatively, an aircraft with conformal tanks and three external drop tanks could undertake a ferry mission, with reserves, from Bitburg AB in Germany to the southern part of the Persian Gulf, a distance of some 2600nm.

An accuracy of between 4 and 8 mils, better than the A-7D Corsair II, F-4E

Phantom or F-111E/F, has been claimed by MCAIR, and CEP (cumulative error probabilities) have ranged between 36ft (11m) and 85ft (26m) using Continuously Displayed Impact Point (CDIP) deliveries in various conditions. These include airspeeds ranging from 420kt to 480kt, dive angles of less than 20deg to more than 40deg, and slant ranges of less than 5,000ft (1,500m) to more than 10,000ft (3,000m). MCAIR also claim to have demonstrated a CEP of 77ft (23·5m) in *blind* bombing, using the F-15B AFCD.

A decision on which of the competing types should be the subject of requests for further funding was due by the end of 1983 and, capabilities apart, the cost factor was certain to influence the selection process. The contract to evaluate

Below: Despite insistence that the FX programme included "not a pound for air-to-ground", high performance, automated systems and a second crew member have made the F-15 a leading candidate for the USAF's dual-role fighter requirement.

Above: The Vought seeker head for the USAF's ASAT missile combines laser gyros, infra-red seekers and rocket motors for satellite tracking.

the capabilities already described was valued at $13 million, and USAF sources indicate that development of an F-15E Eagle to production status would cost in the region of US $350 million, with procurement of the 398 models adding a further $16,000 million.

The basis for the F-15E would be the MSIP-standard F-15D two-seater. To this would be added a fail-operative flight control augmentation system; provision for carrying and launching a variety of weapons, including tactical nuclear bombs; VHF and HF communications; provision for the LANTIRN system, including a modified intertial navigation system, radar altimeter and the Marconi Avionics diffractive-optics, wide-field-of-view HUD; and the new cockpit displays and controls associated with the extra avionics for both pilot and weapons system operator. Additionally, an internal countermeasures set would be installed in the ammunition bay of the F-15E, as two-seat models currently do not carry ECM. Should problems occur with LANTIRN, the Ford Aerospace FLIR pod, derived from that used on the F/A-18 Hornet is available as an alternative, as is the Pave Tack system from the same manufacturer.

Another option for the F-15E, which could come as an MSIP, is the Manoeuvring Attack System, derived from the Integrated Flight and Fire Control/Firefly III developments described in Chapter 4. This would allow weapons to be delivered accurately, or guns fired, during tactical manoeuvring. The first live air-to-air trial of the IFFC took place on August 19, 1982, when an F-15 shot down a PQM-102 target drone over the White Sands Missile Range, New Mexico. The drone was closing at 400kt from a near-frontal position, and both aircraft were in sharp right turns. The

IFFC on the F-15 was activated at a target range of 10,000ft (3,000m) and a closure rate of 760kt, so that in the space of a single two-second burst, comprising 171 rounds of target practice ammunition, target distance shrank from 5,800ft (1,770m) to 3,800ft (1,160m). Under normal circumstances, a fighter has to manoeuvre behind his opponent and open fire from an angle of 30deg or less off the tail. In this case the F-15

attacked from 130deg approaching from the front and right, but the drone was hit and caught fire.

Another planned role for the Eagle is that of satellite killer. While the Soviet Union has been developing its own 'killer' satellites, the United States has adopted a different approach to the problem. In 1979, the Vought Corporation was awarded a US $78.2 million contract to develop an ASAT (anti-satel-

Left: HARM, anti-radar missile, Snakeye bombs, Sparrows and Sidewinders arm the proposed defence suppression Eagle.

Below left: A full-size model of the USAF's ASAT missile ready for loading on an F-15A at Boeing's Seattle facility in August 1982.

lite) system to be operational in 1985. This takes the form of an advanced interceptor missile to be launched from the centreline pylon of an F-15 Eagle, with guidance so accurate that destruction of its target will be by collision, making a warhead unnecessary. Funding of $82.3 million in the FY '80 budget and $268 million in FY '81 was enough for flight testing to continue through 1984.

ASAT system
The ASAT missile is intended to be carried by the F-15 on a pre-directed flight trajectory to the launch point. The missile itself consists of a first stage based on the Boeing AGM-69 Short-Range Attack Missile (SRAM), and a second stage powered by a 6,000lb (2,722kg) thrust Altair III Thikol rocket motor, which for many years has formed the fourth stage of Vought's Scout launch vehicle. A simple seeker combining laser gyros and infra-red sensors operates small rocket motors for course correction during the tracking stage until impact is achieved. Information available by mid-1983 indicated that the ASAT weighs some 2,700kg (1,225kg) and is 17ft 9¾in (5·43m) long and 1ft 7¾in (0·5m) in diameter. Attitude control is provided by two fixed and three movable fins. The F-15 launch pylon incorporates a back-up battery, electrical connections, a communications link, a microprocessor and a gas-generated cartridge ejection unit, and the first two test firings are scheduled by October 1983.

The ASAT programme, also known as

Above: The Boeing-developed ASAT launch pylon incorporates a microprocessor and communications link between missile and aircraft.

the Prototype Miniature Air-launched Segment (PMALS) of the Space Defense Program, is managed by the USAF's Space Command. Boeing Aerospace is responsible for the SRAM first stage, integration services and the missile control centre, while Vought have overall responsibility for the programme as prime contractor and McDonnell Douglas carry out the necessary modifications to the aircraft. A total of 36 F-15s, equipping two squadrons, are expected to be committed to the ASAT role.

A number of other roles have been considered for the F-15C, including tactical reconnaissance and defence suppression to replace the ageing RF-4C and F-4G Wild Weasel variants of the Phantom. However, such developments would be subject to budgeting con-

Below: Vought ASAT is carried by a Space Command Eagle for vibroacoustic trials as part of the captive flight test programme.

Right: The USAF's antisatellite programme involves using the F-15's rapid climb to launch the missile at an altitude of around 80,000ft (24,400m). SRAM first stage and Altair III second stage carry the warhead/seeker to intercept altitude.

siderations. The US House Armed Services Committee in its report on the FY 84 budget request, published in May 1983 quotes the flyaway cost of an F-15C as $25·2 million, compared with $12·78 million for an F-16. The budget request for 48 Eagles in FY 84 was reduced to 30 by Congress, who in addition, "would disapprove multi-year procurement". They feel "there is merit in maintaining two fighter aircraft production lines" for the USAF, and they recommend that F-15 production is maintained at "a minimum sustaining rate". Planned procurement of 696 more F-15s at a total cost of $26 billion, they consider "unaffordable". It is not surprising, therefore, that the same report, when considering tactical fighter derivatives of both the F-15 and F-16, recommends deletion of the $21·4 million requested for long lead items for whichever type is selected.

Glossary and abbreviations

AAA	Anti-aircraft artillery
AAM	Air-to-air missile
AAR	Air-to-air refuelling
AB	US air base (on allied territory)
ADF	Automatic direction finding (system)
ADTAC	Air Defense Tactical Air Command
AFB	US Air Force Base (on sovereign territory)
AFCD	Advanced Fighter Capability Demonstrator (ex-Strike Eagle)
AGM-	US designation for air-to-ground missile
AIM-	US designation for air intercept missile
AIS	Avionics intermediate shop
AMRAAM	Advanced medium-range air-to-air missile
analogue	Electronic system in which quantities are represented by electrical signals of variable characteristics, i.e. by electrical analogues
anhedral	Angle of wing, canard or tailplane below horizontal
ARI	Aileron-rudder interconnect
ASAT	Anti-satellite (missile system)
aspect ratio	Wing slenderness in plan form, numerically span^2/area
ASRAAM	Advanced short range air-to-air missile
ASW	Anti-submarine warfare
augmentation	afterburning (reheat)
AWACS	Airborne warning and control system (Boeing E-3A Sentry)
BIT(E)	Built-in test (equipment)
BVR	Beyond visual range
bypass ratio	Ratio of total airflow through a turbofan engine to that passing through the core section
camber	Curvature of the centreline of a wing aerofoil
CAS	Control augmentation system
CDIP	Continuously displayed impact point
CEP	Circular error probability
CFS	Concept formulation study
chord	Imaginary line joining the leading and trailing edges of a wing or aerofoil section
clutter	Spurious returns on a radar scope
CRT	Cathode ray tube
CW	Continuous-wave radiation
DCP	Development concept paper
DFE	Derivative fighter engine (now the GE F110)
digital	Electronic system in which quantities are as on/off signals coded to represent numbers
dihedral	Angle of wing, canard or tailplane above the horizontal
Doppler	Radar which measures changes in frequency between reflections in the

	ground ahead of and behind the aircraft, thus giving accurate measure of speed over the ground; Doppler effect is also used to pick out moving targets.
DTD	Damage tolerant design
ECCM	Electronic counter-countermeasures
ECM	Electronic countermeasures
ECP	Engineering change proposals
EO	Electro-optical
EW	Electronic warfare
FAST packs	Fuel and sensor tactical packs (also known as conformal tanks)
FIS	Fighter interception squadron
FLAMR	Forward looking multi-mode radar
FLIR	Forward looking infra-red
FSD	Full scale development
FWW	Fighter weapons wing
FY	Fiscal year (as in US budgets)
g	Acceleration due to standard gravity, unit of linear acceleration
GE	General Electric Company (USA)
GHz	GigaHertz (Hertz × 1,000,000,000)
GPS	Global positioning system
HF	High frequency
HUD	Head-up display
Hz	Hertz, cycles per second
IDFAF	Israeli Defence Force – Air Force
ILS	Instrument landing system
INS	Inertial navigation system
IR	Infra-red, heat radiation
JASDF	Japanese Air Self-Defense Force
JTIDS	Joint tactical information distribution system
KHz	Kilo Hertz (Hertz × 1000)
LANTIRN	Low-altitude navigation and targeting infra-red for night
LLTV	Low-light television
LRU	Line replaceable unit
Mach	Unit equal to the speed of sound
Maple Flag	Series of tactical air exercises carried out over Canada in as realistic manner as possible, including EW
MCAIR	McDonnell Aircraft Company (part of the McDonnell Douglas Corporation)
MMH/FH	Maintenance man hours per flight hour
MSIP	Multi-staged improvement programme
MTBF	Mean time between failure
MW	Megawatt
NDT	Non-destructive testing

PACAF	US Pacific Air Force
Pave Tack	FLIR sensor/laser designator system carried on F-111F and F-4 Phantom, and tested on F-15; produced by Ford Aerospace
PRF	Pulse repetition frequency
PSP	Programmable signal processor
P&W	Pratt & Whitney
Red Flag	Series of tactical air exercises carried out in Nevada in as realistic manner as possible, including EW
RFP	Requests for proposals
RoKAF	Republic of Korea Air Force
RSAF	Royal Saudi Air Force
RWR	Radar warning receiver
R&D	Research and development
SAM	Surface-to-air missile
SAR	Synthetic aperture radar
Seek Talk	Codename for a secure communications system under development
semi-active	Homing on radiation reflected from a target illuminated by radar carried in fighter or other vehicle (but not the missile itself)
slick	Streamlined (Aero-1A shape) bomb
SPR	Sortie production rate
SRAM	Short range attack missile
TAC	USAF Tactical Air Command
TACAN	Tactical air navigation
TEWS	Tactical electronic warfare system
TFS	Tactical fighter squadron
TFTS	Tactical fighter training squadron
TFTW	Tactical fighter training wing
TFW	Tactical fighter wing
UHF	Ultra-high frequency
USAF	United States Air Force
VFAX	Project designation for a carrier-based fighter/attack aircraft
VFX	Project designation for a carrier-based fighter aircraft
VHF	Very-high frequency
Wild Weasel	Codename for defence-suppression aircraft (as in F-4G Wild Weasel)
wing loading	Aircraft weight divided by wing area
'Zulu' alert	Aircraft maintained on constant readiness to scramble against unidentified air targets 365 days a year

Specifications

	F-15A	F-15C
Length	63ft 9in/10.43m	63ft 9in/10.43m
Wingspan	42ft 9¾in/13.05m	42ft 9¾in/13.05m
Height	18ft 5½in/5.63m	18ft 5½in/5.63m
Weights		
Empty	28,000lb/12,700kg	28,000lb/12,700kg
Takeoff (air-to-air)	41,500lb/18,824kg	44,500lb/20,185kg
Maximum takeoff	56,000lb/25,401kg	68,000lb/30,844kg
Wing area	608sq ft/56.5sq m	608sq ft/56.5sq m
Load factor	+9g/−3g	+9g/−3g
Combat thrust:weight ratio	1.4:1	1.3:1
Maximum speed	>Mach2.5	>Mach2.5
Service ceiling	65,000ft/19,813m	65,000ft/19,813m
Range		
Ferry (with external tanks)	>2,500nm/4,630km	>2,500nm/4,630km
Ferry (with FAST Packs)	—	>3,000nm/5,556km
Internal fuel	11,635lb/5,278kg	13,455lb/6,103kg
Number of hardpoints	5	5
Maximum ordnance load	16,000lb/7,257kg	16,000lb/7,257kg

Picture credits

PRINTED IN BELGIUM BY

proost
INTERNATIONAL BOOK PRODUCTION